SKETCHES IN THE

EVOLUTION OF ENGLISH
CONGREGATIONALISM

SKETCHES IN THE

EVOLUTION OF ENGLISH CONGREGATIONALISM

Carew Lecture for 1900–01

DELIVERED IN

HARTFORD THEOLOGICAL SEMINARY CONNECTICUT

By ALEXANDER MACKENNAL, D.D.

Author of
"The Story of the English Separatists," "Homes and Haunts of the Pilgrim Fathers," &c.

London
JAMES NISBET & CO., LIMITED
21 BERNERS STREET
1901

Printed by BALLANTYNE, HANSON & Co.
At the Ballantyne Press

TO THE REV. CHESTER D. HARTRANFT
AND THE FACULTY HE PRESIDES OVER
THIS VOLUME IS DEDICATED IN
ADMIRATION OF THEIR WORK AND
REMEMBRANCE OF THEIR FRIENDSHIP

Preface

THE Carew Lecture was founded in the year 1873, to enable "occasional instruction" to be given to the students of the Theological Institute of Connecticut, now the Hartford Theological Seminary; and the trust provided that the Lectures be open to the public.

The object of the present Lecture is to "instruct the students" and others as to the spiritual forces and conditions which have made English Congregationalism what it is to-day; giving only so much of the history as would make the course of the development clear.

The Lecturer believes that as many Englishmen as Americans will be interested in this special treatment of his theme.

The subjects sketched, and the proportion observed in their treatment, have been partly determined by the fact that the Lecturer had in view an American audience and English readers.

In treating of Robert Browne and his contemporaries, it has not been found possible to avoid saying over again some things already said in "The Story of the English Separatists." The quotation on pages 70 and 71 is from that book.

Contents

LECTURE I

PAGE

THE PROBLEM OF THE ENGLISH REFORMATION . . 1

LECTURE II

CONGREGATIONALISM BEFORE ROBERT BROWNE . . 41

LECTURE III

PRESBYTERIANS AND INDEPENDENTS 83

LECTURE IV

REACTIONS AND REVIVAL 125

LECTURE V

CONGREGATIONALISTS AND ANGLICANS 167

LECTURE VI

SEVENTEENTH CENTURY INDEPENDENTS AND TWENTIETH
CENTURY CONGREGATIONALISTS . . . 213

LECTURE I

THE PROBLEM OF THE ENGLISH REFORMATION

Archbishop Sandys's perplexity—The Primitive Church
and Tudor England—Sandys's Protestantism—His Courage
—Residence in Strasburg—His Return to England—Church
Preferment under Elizabeth—The Sorrows of Preferment—
The Reformer thwarted by the Queen—Sandys's Self-dis-
satisfaction—Archbishop Grindal also an Uneasy Man—
Reason of their Inconsistency—Conscience and Patriotism—
Sir Edwin Sandys's *Europæ Speculum*—Power of Calvinism
—Calvinism as an Ecclesiastical System—Ecclesiastical
Calvinism and English Puritanism—Thomas Cartwright—
Fruitless Efforts of Puritans to direct the English Reforma-
tion—" Why did they remain in the Church ?"—Conscience
and Patriotism—The Conscience of the Separatists—Their
Patriotism — The Separatists were true Englishmen —
Nationalists, Puritans, and Separatists contribute to Eng-
lish Progress—The Political Foresight of the Separatists—
M. Borgeaud on the *Mayflower* Compact.

LECTURE I

THE PROBLEM OF THE ENGLISH REFORMATION

I

ARCHBISHOP SANDYS, under whose son, Sir Samuel Sandys, Elder Brewster and his father occupied the mansion-house of Scroby, wrote the following words in the preamble to his will: "The state of a small private church, and the form of a learned Christian kingdom, neither would long like nor can at all brook one and the same ecclesiastical government." The sentence will appear to some a truism; others will think it oracular, and suspect its motive; we may even fancy it to be one of those epigrams in which a clever man suggests an excuse for occupying a position he is not satisfied with. Standing, however, in his solemn will and testament, dated not quite a year before his death, and read in connection with the whole preamble, the words are not without a certain pathos.

Sandys began his public life a zealous and thorough-going Protestant Reformer. He was Vice-Chancellor of the University of Cambridge in the hopeful days of King Edward VI., and pressed for the removal of everything that savoured of Popery in the English Church. At Edward's death he preached a sermon on the proclamation of the Lady Jane Grey as queen; hoping that her accession would secure the triumph of Protestantism. Two days after, when he was sending off his sermon to London for printing, a university "bedellus" "came weeping to him, and prayed him to shift for himself," for Queen Mary was proclaimed. He knew that his life was in danger; but "he was not troubled herewithal," says his contemporary Fox, "for he had ever a man's courage, and could not be terrified." "My life," he affirmed, "is not dear unto me, neither have I done or said anything that urgeth my conscience. For that which I spoke of the State I have instructions warranted by the subscription of sixteen counsellors; neither can speech be treason, neither yet have I spoken further than the Word of God and the laws of the realm doth warrant me, come of me what God will."

After an imprisonment of many weeks he went away to Antwerp, only just escaping the officers who were sent to reapprehend him, and who saw the sails of the ship that was carrying him off. King Philip of Spain, Mary's affianced husband, searched Antwerp for him, and Sandys went to Strasburg. While making this his home for a season, he sought acquaintance with some Continental Reformers, Peter Martyr and Bullinger among them. He was in Peter Martyr's house when word was brought him that Queen Mary had died. "He took his leave, and returned to Strausborough, where he preached, and so Master Grindall and he came towards England, and came to London the same day that Queen Elizabeth was crowned."

His Protestant zeal had been refreshed by four years' intercourse with the Continental Reformers; it was tempered by his knowledge of causes of dissension among the English congregations in Germany and Switzerland; but he was full of hope for England under the new queen. Elizabeth received him graciously, and made him one of her commissioners for revising the Common Prayer; in other ways he was soon fully employed about the reformation of religion. He hesitated in accepting a bishopric, because of his dislike of the vestments of the priesthood and the ornaments of public worship. After he was consecrated Bishop of Worcester he almost lost his preferment by opposing the Queen, who retained the crucifix in her private chapel, and was for keeping this symbol and images of the saints in the churches. " As to myself," he writes Peter Martyr, " because I was rather vehement in this matter, and could by no means consent that an occasion of stumbling should be afforded to the Church of Christ, I was very near being deposed from my office and incurring the displeasure of the Queen. But God, in whose hand are the hearts of kings, gave us tranquillity instead of a tempest, and delivered the Church of England from stumbling-blocks of this kind; only the popish vestments remain in our Church—I mean the copes, which, however, we hope will not last very long." He spoke from his See against the compulsory imposition of conformity; he declared that "the bishops would give up their livings rather than swear that the Queen was supreme head of the Church;" in the Convocation of 1562 he presented a paper recommending the adoption of an improved system of ecclesiastical government and discipline. So brave were his beginnings.

From Worcester he was removed to the more important See of London, following Grindal, who had been made Archbishop of York. And when Grindal was promoted to Canterbury in 1576, he again succeeded him as Archbishop of York. He held this preferment twelve years; the whole length of his Episcopate was nearly thirty years. He died "Primate of England"; it was thought he would have been made Archbishop of Canterbury and "Primate of all England" when Grindal died. But his warmth of temper was a difficulty; there was another difficulty in Queen Elizabeth's reluctance to make a married man the first ecclesiastical personage of the realm.

Sandys was well able to appreciate his successes. He was born in a Cumbrian hall; his mother was a descendant of the ancient barons of Kendal. He was of the class of old English gentry who think that their ancestry and local influence make them at least the equals of the aristocracy. It is a class which has given many members to the higher ranks in the Church and in the law, who take precedence among peers. His family is still connected with Hawkshead, where the archbishop founded the grammar-school in which the "poet's mind" awoke in Wordsworth, and there Sandys's portrait is to be seen. But his prosperity did not bring him happiness. He found himself entangled in the perplexities of high life, and could not always get men to see that he was walking straight. Before he was fully installed in the archbishopric he had to resist an attempt by the Crown to acquire the palace of Bishopthorp. Then came a disagreement with Grindal about dilapidations, which are so serious a charge on all English benefices. He quarrelled with Aylmer, his successor in the See of London, over both dilapidations and arrears. The Queen wished him to grant her a lease of Scroby Manor, an appanage of the Archbishopric of York, and he refused because of the injury which would be done to the See. The loss would be many thousands of pounds—"too much, Most Gracious Sovereign, too much to pull from a bishoprick inferior to many others in revenue, but superior in charge and countenance." A month after writing this letter he leased the manor to his son for a rent of £65, 6s. 8d. Of course his inconsistency was commented on. "He was the first Protestant bishop," says Mr. Hunter,[1] "who raised a powerful family out of the goods of the Church." Six sons enjoyed leases of the episcopal lands. They were men of merit, and they won distinction; their eminence kept people mindful of the start their father had given them in life. Sandys was, moreover, a passionate man, and made enemies; plots were laid for him, and malignant charges brought against him.

He does not refer to any of these matters in his will, but he is very anxious to clear himself from the suspicion of insincerity or time-serving. His earnestness betokens a heart ill at ease, if not a troubled conscience. "Because I have lived an old man in the ministry of Christ, a faithful disposer of the mysteries

---

[1] "The Founders of New Plymouth," by the Rev. Joseph Hunter, F.S.A.L. London: John Russell Smith, 1854. P. 22.

of God and to my power an earnest labourer in the vineyard of the Lord, I testify before God and His angels and men of this world I rest resolute and yield up my spirit in that doctrine which I have privately studied and publicly preached, and which is this day maintained in the Church of England. . . . I have not laboured to please man, but studied to please my Master, who sent me not to flatter either prince or people. . . . Concerning rites and ceremonies by political constitutions authorised among us, as I am and have been persuaded that such as are now set down by public authority in this Church of England are no way either ungodly or unlawful, but may with good conscience, for order and obedience' sake, be used of a good Christian . . . so have I ever been, and presently am persuaded that some of them be not so expedient in this Church now, but that in the Church reformed, and in all this time of the Gospel (wherein the seed of the Scripture hath so long been sown), they may better be disused by little and little than more and more urged." A reference to the Puritans follows, in which is the sentence quoted at the beginning of this Lecture :

"Howbeit, as I do easily acknowledge our
ecclesiastical policy in some points may be
bettered, so do I utterly mislike, even in my
conscience, all such rude and indigested platforms as have been more lately and boldly than
either learnedly or wisely preferred, tending
not to the reformation, but to the destruction
of the Church of England. The particularities
of both sorts [doctrine and discipline] reserved
to the discretion of the godly wise, of the latter
I only say thus, that the state of a small
private church, and the form of a learned
Christian kingdom, neither would long like nor
can at all brook one and the same ecclesiastical government." "Thus much," he continues,
"I thought good to testify concerning these
ecclesiastical matters, to clear me from all
suspicion of double and indirect dealing in
the house of God, wherein as touching mine
office I have not halted, but walked sincerely
according to that skill and ability which I
received at God's merciful hands. Lord, as
a great sinner by reason of my frail flesh
and manifold infirmities, I flee unto Thee
for mercy. Lord, forgive me my sins, for
I acknowledge my sins. Lord, perform Thy

promise, and do away all mine iniquities. Haste the coming of Thy Christ, and deliver me from this body of sin : *Veni cito, Domine Jesu.* Clothe me with immortality, and give that promised crown of glory. So be it."

Archbishop Sandys was by no means an exceptional personage among the ecclesiastical dignitaries of that time. The Queen appointed with him as her first bishops, Jewel, Grindal, Horn, Cox, Parkhurst, and Bentham. They were all men pledged to the religious Reformation, which Wyclif had begun ; which Henry VIII., without intending it, reinvigorated ; which was advanced by Edward VI. ; opposed by Mary Tudor ; and ultimately checked by the imperious temper and autocratic rule of Elizabeth. They remonstrated with the Queen, and exhorted Parliament to do away with all the remnants of Popery in worship, to grant some liberty to conscience, to encourage evangelical preaching ; their language was sometimes vehement, it always has the tone of sincerity. They were equally concerned over the assumption by the Queen's courts of authority to determine the practice of the clergy and the discipline of the

Church. The Zurich Letters are full of lamentations about their pitiable plight. Jewel writes: "As heretofore Christ was cast out by His enemies, so He is now kept out by His friends." "That little cross of ill omen still maintains its place in the Queen's chapel. Wretched me! this thing will soon be drawn into a precedent." "I wish that all, even the slightest vestiges, of Popery might be removed from our churches and, above all, from our minds. But the Queen will not endure the least alteration in matters of religion." Grindal and Horn, in a joint letter to Bullinger and Gualter, say: "We most solemnly make oath that we have hitherto laboured with all earnestness, fidelity, and diligence to effect what our brethren require. But now we are brought into such straits, what is to be done we leave you to conjecture; but since we cannot do what we would, we should do in the Lord what we can." "Although we are unable to remove all the abuses of this fiscal court, as also some others, yet we do not cease to find fault with and censure them, and send them back to that hell from whence they proceeded." These strong words are associated with others in which they try to justify their

conformity: they speak of the necessity of their
continuing in office and conciliating the Queen;
their fear lest public disputing should alienate
the minds of the nobility, and encourage the
papal party; and they declare that, in their
administration of their bishoprics, they leave
every minister "at liberty to speak against all
matters of this kind, [so as it is done] with
modesty and sobriety"; "we by no means de-
prive of their office those ministers who refuse
to receive or approve of those articles falsely
ascribed to us." They would have been glad
if they could have won from Peter Martyr,
Bullinger, and Gualter even a qualified approval
of a position which they felt so burdensome
to their conscience.

Between Grindal and the Queen there was
at last an open rupture. He had not been at
Canterbury a year when Elizabeth ordered him
to suppress the "prophesyings," or public preach-
ings, in assemblies specially gathered for the
purpose. "She thought these meetings gave
encouragement to novelty"; that people's
"curiosity was too much indulged, and their
heads overcharged with notions, by these discourses." She did not love appeals to the

public of any sort, fearing national disturbance. She thought that three or four preachers in a county might be enough; and that homilies, prepared for the clergy, should be read by them instead of their using free speech. Grindal, who would have had every minister a preacher, able to deliver his own discourses, refused to comply, and wrote a long letter to Elizabeth on the subject. Thomas Fuller has commented on this letter: "What could be written with more spirit or less animosity, more humility and less dejection? I see a lamb in his own can be a lion in God and his Church's cause." "All the archbishop could say or write," to quote Strype, "moved not the Queen from her resolution; but she seemed much offended with him, and resolved to have him suspended and sequestered; and seeing he would not be instrumental in it, sent her own commandment, by her letters, to the rest of the bishops, wholly to put down the exercises." Grindal was advised by the Lord Treasurer Burleigh to submit to the Queen, but he would not; he had done nothing amiss, he said, and refused to ask pardon which supposed a fault. The opinion of the Queen's counsellors was against depriving him of his office, but he continued either wholly, or in part, disabled from the exercise of it. It is creditable to Whitgift, who was nominated as his successor, that he would not enter on the See while Grindal was alive. Thomas Fuller gives us a last picture of him : " Being really blind, more with grief than age, he was willing to put off his clothes before he went to bed, and in his lifetime to resign his place to Dr. Whitgift, who refused such accept- ance thereof. And the Queen, commiserating his condition, was graciously pleased to say, that as she had made him, so he should die an archbishop; as he did, July 6, 1583. Worldly wealth he cared not for, desiring only to make both ends meet; and as for that little that lapped over, he gave it to pious uses in both universities, and the founding of a fair free - school at St. Bees, the place of his nativity."

The most pathetic object on which we can look is the troubled conscience of good men in a false position. When we read Sandys's *Apologia*, and see Grindal passing out of the world in name only an archbishop, we are

sure to ask ourselves—How could such men
have borne it? Compromising with themselves
and ill at ease, failing to retain the confidence
of persons who had trusted them and whose
approval they valued, seeing the inevitable
drift of things, the cause for which they were
sacrificing so much losing ground daily, the
popish errors they called hellish, and Antichrist, daily becoming more familiar to Protestants, and securing hold on the life of the
nation—why did they not assert the freedom
of Christian men, break away from their en-
tanglements, and labour directly for the full
Reformation which was so dear to them? It
is easy to call them cowards and time-servers;
easy to speak of "loaves and fishes," social
recognition, Court favour, love of power. But
we make a great mistake if we think it is only
a good man's worse self that leads him astray;
quite as often he errs by a false reading of
the good.

Two motives seem to me to have been
dominant in them—conscience and patriotism.
These men had a high sense of the sanctity of
their orders. They had been called into the
ministry by God, and they were under respon-

sibility to God to exercise their ministry, if it
was in any wise possible for them honestly to
do so. They were able men; many of them
had been exiles in the cause of Protestantism.
In Frankfort, Strasburg, Zurich, they came into
association with others like themselves, strong,
zealous, masterful persons, whose counsel and
sympathy confirmed their belief that they were
called to be instruments of Reformation in
England. They came back full of hope, ready
to take a difficult post in accomplishing their
mission. The sense of their responsibility became more and more urgent the harder they
found their task; and when it proved an impossible enterprise, it was too late to draw
back. Their patriotism, too, was a plea they
could not resist. There was still a popish
clergy in England; probably a majority of the
priests they found in office were in heart Catholics of the Roman type. That clergy would
have furnished and trained bishops had these
retired. And a perpetual protest on their part,
constant resistance of the Queen, whom they
were fain to believe God's appointed bulwark
of Protestantism, ceaseless strife in the councils
of the realm, seemed to them certain to end

in social disruption, perhaps in civil war. The true problem of the Reformation in England was — how to secure purity in doctrine and worship without rending the nation asunder; it was to bring back the simplicity and sanctity of the Apostolic Church in a land which had grown complex in condition, with a history it could not break from, and containing many citizens who desired no Reformation.

II

THE most eminent of Archbishop Sandys's children was his second son, Sir Edwin, mentioned in Bradford's "History of Plymouth Plantation" as the friend of the Pilgrim Fathers, the treasurer and governor of the Virginia Company. When a young man, while his brother George was pursuing his classical studies in the East, he was travelling in Western Europe, trying to understand the Roman controversy and the relations of the Protestant sects to one another, with a view to see how they might be brought into a "unitie universalle." His report, intended for presentation to an ecclesiastical dignitary, was published fifteen years after without his authority, under the title *Europæ Speculum*. It is a judicious book—Sir Edwin had been a pupil of Richard Hooker—a book full of keen observation, philosophic reflections, and grave humour, breathing throughout a generous spirit. Among other things, he tells us that his original view of the Roman Church, gained by speculation, was not nearly so unfavourable as his later judgment, formed by actual examination. He also says that, " of all places, the desires and attempts [of the Papists] to recover England, have been always and still are the strongest;" which, " in theyr more sober moods, sundry of them will acknowledge to have been the only nation that took the right way of justificall Reformation, in comparison of other who have runne headlong rather to a tumultuous innovation (so they conceive it). Whereas that alteration which hath been in England, was brought in with peaceable and orderly proceeding, by generall consent of the Prince and whole Realme representatively assembled in solemn Parliament, a great part of their owne Clergie according and conforming themselves with it ; no Luther, no Calvin, in the

square of theyr Faith." There is one significant passage in his description of the hostility
of the Romanists to all religious communities
but their own. "Theyr hatred is to the
Lutheran, the author of theyr calamitie; but
hatred and feare both of the Calvinist onely,
whom they accompt the only growing enemie
and dangerous to their state. For as for the
Lutheran, hee was long since at his highest;
and if he itch an inch forward one way for an
ell he loseth an other."

Sir Edwin's discovery of the tenacious vigour
of Calvinism had been anticipated half a century before by many English Reformers. When
Dr. Cox went over to Frankfort, where, in the
time of Mary's persecution, a church of our
countrymen was gathered, under licence of the
magistrates, he found it established on a Calvinistic basis; his endeavours to re-establish
it on that moderate platform, which gratified
so many Papists, was the reason of "the troubles
in Frankfort." The moderate and the thorough-
going Reformers both foresaw that, when the
Protestant Princess Elizabeth ascended the
throne, and the exiles returned, the influence
of the Continental churches would be felt

in the settlement of religion in their own
country; hence the vehemence of the controversy between them. The congregation had
the sympathy of Calvin himself and the
Zurich Reformers; they were in correspond-
ence with the Cambridge Protestants at home.
They vainly appealed to Sandys, and some
others who afterward were made bishops, to
help them in thwarting Cox's schemes. They
would have smiled had the future archbishop
spoken to them of the distinction between
" a small private church" and the church of "a
learned Christian kingdom;" it was not only
the little Frankfort congregation they were
zealous for, but the Church of England as it
was to be.

Here we must distinguish between Calvinism
as a theological doctrine and Calvinism as an
ecclesiastical system. When we talk of Calvinism to-day, we mean the doctrine of predestina-
tion, with its corollaries of personal election,
effectual calling, and the perseverance of the
saints. There was no controversy among the
English Reformers about this; it was the doctrine common to Protestants. Even Whitgift
was a Calvinist in this sense; so were the

men who afterward broke away from the
Puritans: Barrowe was a Calvinist, and John
Robinson; Henry Ainsworth bases his Congregationalism on the doctrine of personal election.
The ecclesiastical system of Calvinism is as
really a State-church doctrine as is the Anglican
system, but with this profound difference.
The English Church has always and inevitably
tended to Erastianism; the Church is regarded
as the nation in its religious aspect and func-
tions. Lord Rosebery has expressed the doctrine bluntly: "I believe a State has as much
right to sustain a standing Church as it has to
sustain a standing army." Calvinism recognises
the Church as a distinct body constituted by
direct divine calling, and believes that God intended it to regulate the faith and morals of
the people. In England, whenever it has been
feared that serious social complications would result from carrying out the principles of the New
Testament, political necessity has determined the
issue; the Church has had to give way to the
Crown. Calvin, on the other hand, governed
Geneva. The Calvinistic system means the
interference of the Church with the life of the
nation, the direction of its faith and morals

by ministers and elders of the Church—consistories, classes, presbyteries, and synods.

The Church at Frankfort, while glad to have the sympathy of the Continental Calvinists, had not adopted—there was no occasion that it should adopt—the full Calvinistic ecclesiastical sytem; indeed there are some things in its action, as we shall see hereafter, which look rather to Congregationalism than to Presbyterianism. But the most prominent leader of the Puritan party, which Church historians affiliate to the Geneva Church, did adopt it. Thomas Cartwright, Fellow of St. John's College, Cambridge, and Lady Margaret Professor of Divinity, whose "pulpit exercises were so much followed that, when he preached at St. Mary's [the university] Church, the windows of the church were taken down for the accommodation of the multitudes who flocked to hear him," goes so far as to make clerical authority of the essence of the Church. The well-known XIXth Article of the Church of England, "on the Church," so admirable for its catholicity, was issued by authority of King Edward in 1553, the second year before his death. It reads: "The visible Church of

Christ is a congregation of faithful men, in
which the pure Word of God is preached, and
the Sacraments be duly administered, according
to Christ's ordinance, in all those things that
of necessity are requisite to the same." The
Frankfort congregation evidently accepts this
article, but makes a significant addition to it
concerning fellowship. " What thing ought
we to have in greater recommendation than
the Order and Policy which God hath established in His Church? that we may be taught
by his Word, that we may worship him and
call on his name with one accord, that we may
have the true use of the Sacraments to help
us to the same?" And again : " We have a
Church freely granted to preach God's Word
purely, to minister the Sacraments sincerely,
and to execute Discipline truly." Cartwright,
however, makes this sweeping affirmation :
" Without any part of that Order or Discipline which the Lord hath appointed, I grant
there can be no Church of Christ; or, that
without some part of it, there can be no faith
in Jesus Christ. It is a part of the Discipline
of our Saviour Christ that there should be
certain which should be chosen out of the

rest to preach the gospel, by preaching whereof
the Churches are gathered together. Where,
therefore, there is no ministry of the Word,
there it is plain that there are no visible and
apparent Churches. It is another piece of the
Discipline of the Lord that the rest of the body
should obey them that are set over them in
the Lord ; wherever, therefore, there is no
obedience of the people to the ministers that
in the Lord's name preach unto them, there
can be no true Church of Christ."

The Puritan was a man of immense moral
courage. No *reductio ad absurdum* made him
halt in his logic; neither scorn nor indifference
could abash him in maintaining his points.
When he undertook the charge of the nation
nothing was too small for him to look after,
nothing too great for him to attempt. He
could cut down a maypole with Endicott at
Merry Mount and the Martindales at Rostherne ; he could make Mary Queen of Scots
tremble in her closet; and compare Queen
Elizabeth, in a Court sermon, to an untamed
heifer. It was with no light heart he assumed
the regulation of public faith and morals; he
was aware of the responsibility, and it made him

a grave man. He had indomitable patience; for a hundred and thirty-five years, from "the troubles at Frankfort," in 1554, to the passing of the Toleration Act in 1689, he fought his battle, always being worsted, but never accepting his defeat. Friends fell away from him, he enjoyed no more of the favour of the Court than if he had been a confessed dissenter; he made the prophets of the Old Testament his companions, and yet there was in him a fountain of sweetness drawn from the gospel. He was tender to the poor, gentle in the sick-room, a sympathetic counsellor to weak and troubled consciences. The beautiful hymn bearing Baxter's name—

> " Lord, it belongs not to my share
> Whether I die or live "—

is a cento from a poem the old man wrote to comfort a girl in spiritual depression, and forms part of one of the purest and most romantic love-stories in English literature. "Endurance" was the Puritan's "crowning quality." He stayed himself on the compassion and fidelity of Him who numbereth the very hairs of His people's heads, telleth their wanderings, puts their tears into His bottle, and writes them in His book. The pragmatism, the portentous solemnity, and the obstinacy, which form the main features of his character in popular histories and novels, are but the caricatures of his noble qualities. There were hypocrites among the Puritans, but the Puritan was no hypocrite. He would often unwittingly caricature himself, but he held fast his profession until death.

Speaking of the painful position of Sandys and Grindal, I have asked—How could they bear it? with still more emphasis I ask myself —How could the Puritans bear theirs? From the days of Elizabeth to the days of Charles II., a hundred years, with the exception of the short period of the Commonwealth, they were Nonconformists within the Established Church, and they must have found it an irksome state. It wounded their self-respect; they were fretted and hindered in their preaching and their parish work, dependent on the casual toleration of a few friendly bishops and lay patrons, who stood between them and the Crown. The Separatists set them the example of forming churches, in which, when they were able to meet, their worship was according to the order they themselves had laid down, and all their hearers were sympathetic. But the Puritans stayed where they were; they would not leave the Church of England. They were persecuted, admonished, checked, but they remained. James talked of harrying them out of the Church, or worse, if they would not conform; but James's vanity was no match for the pride in patience of the Puritans: they neither conformed nor separated. They did not go until they were put out by a new law —Charles II.'s Act of Uniformity in 1662.

The animating principles of their fortitude were those which justified the bishop's party in their conformity—their conscience and their patriotism. All through their controversies their reverence for their ministerial office appears. They were called of God to their various charges; their ordination had been to service in the Established Church. They had a high sense of their duty to their nation; God had blessed England with the dawn of a Reformation, and though the dawn had been obscured and clouded, it was for them to wait on Him until the clouds should lift. Scottish

Presbyterianism shows us this Puritan sentiment of the sanctity of national religion at
its highest. Not until our own times has the
Free Church of Scotland, the representative
of the old evangelical theology of the first
Reformers, recognised that a nation may be
Christian without an Established Church.
There are Scotsmen even now who believe
that Scotland is a covenanted nation, and the
Reformed Presbyterian Church in the United
States inherits the tradition. "Why should
there be such a Church here?" I said a few
years ago to a minister who had sprung from
that stock. "America is surely not included
in the Scottish covenant." His answer was
striking : "The Reformed Presbyterian Church,"
he said, "stands for the moral personality of
the nation." English Presbyterianism never
soared to the height of that great argument;
but it was charged with the sense of national
Christian obligation, national Protestant obligation, and it knew no way of fulfilling it
but to labour for a wholly Reformed and purely
Protestant National Church. The Puritans
were ready to wait as well as to labour. They
would tarry for prince, would tarry for people,

but they could not abate their ideal; they could neither conform to the established order nor voluntarily quit their Church.

III

The conscientiousness of the Separatists—the men who, tired at length of tarrying for a Reformation which the Puritans were always promising, but which never came, broke away altogether from the Established Church—needs no defence before those whom I am addressing; indeed, it has never been challenged seriously by any. The scores who died in London prisons, and the three men—Henry Barrowe, John Greenwood, and John Penry—who were so wantonly hanged at Tyburn, were martyrs for conscience' sake. The ceaseless endurance of suffering and ignominy by the London church, and their banishment to Holland, the vexation and harassment of the churches in Gainsborough and Scroby, and their exile in the same place of refuge, witnessed to the sustaining power of conscience. It was the "rude grasp" of conscience which drove the Pilgrim Fathers across the sea; the broken - hearted remnants of the fellowship in Amsterdam, who dribbled back to London, there haply to accomplish the work of settling a pure and peaceful Church, which they had failed to do in their exile, were under the same constraint. The Church in the Catacombs did not contain truer-souled men than Ainsworth and Jacob, and others whose names are lost; perhaps, if the inner history of the early Roman Christians were as fully known as we know that of Amsterdam, we should find there too some miserable details, sullying the record, but not availing to destroy the impression of fidelity.

What has not been so fully recognised in the history of the Separatists is that their patriotism, though different in aim, was not a whit inferior in quality to that of the Puritans and the Anglicans. Their first concern is with the Churches; that they be constituted and governed according to the will of Christ; that the members be disciplined in faith and knowledge and godly character; but it is clear that they believed that in seeking this they were labouring for the welfare of the nation. One of the most touching features in the prison conferences between the suffering Separatists and the Royal Commissioners sent to interrogate them is the constant appeal of the prisoners for public debate, regularly conducted, carefully taken down and reported without partial editing. They long to get at the ear of England; they are confident that both their personal integrity and the soundness of their cause will appeal to their fellow-countrymen if only they be fairly listened to.

The same confidence appears in some "motions touching Unitie, sent by a few who are falselie and maliciouslie called Brownistes." A portion of it was written by Barrowe; within a month of his execution the troubled Church enlarges his appeal and prepares it for private circulation to the Lord Mayor and Counsellors of London, to the Judges and Counsellors of the realm. In a document preserved in the British Museum,[1] one of the sheets is endorsed " Penry ye othur " (author), and the style—fervid, vacillating, and absolutely sincere — is like his. A third person—a redactor—apparently an uneducated man, has gone over the sheets, correcting and adding to the work of the martyrs. It is an impassioned appeal,

[1] Harleian MSS., 6848, Article i.

C

shewing how cruelly the blow which had fallen
on the Church was afflicting them, and containing some touching details of their sufferings.
Equally impassioned is the confidence it displays in English fairplay; the petitioners do
not believe that anything but misconception
can account for the injustice they are enduring.
"For God's sake, for Queen Elizabeth's sake,
for England's sake, and for your own sake,"
they appeal, "peruse it with favour. It ten-
deth to Mercy and Unity." There is no word
of retractation in the appeal, but an intense
desire to be reconciled to their fellow-countrymen, and an unfaltering confidence that they
would be left in peace to follow conscience if
they were but understood.

Nor was this patriotism an evanescent feeling. It characterises the whole history of the
Independents; it saved them from cherishing
scorn of England, and mitigated the bitterness
of their lot. Only patriots could have founded
the Plymouth Colony, and given form to the
United States. It was patriotism to which
Cromwell appealed when he made of the
humble men of these Churches an army, able
to "encounter gentlemen, that have honour

and courage and resolution in them." "I raised," he said, "such men as had the fear of God before them, as made some conscience of what they did; and from that day forward, I must say to you, they were never beaten, and wherever they were engaged against the enemy, they beat continually."

The Separatists were Englishmen, with the English prejudice against foreigners, the English intensity of purpose.

Robinson's company could not become Dutchmen; could they have done so, they would have made happy homes in Leyden, or established a colony under the protection of Holland, and their condition would have been far easier than it was under the lee of Cape Cod, with James Stuart as their king. It was to found a new England that the *Mayflower* left the old shores. To help in making a new England was equally the task of those who stayed in the mother-land. The England of to-day is as different from Tudor England, and the England of the early Stuarts, as is America from Great Britain; nay, the difference is far greater, and the work of my forefathers, since the seventeenth century, was quite as arduous as that of yours. Limited monarchy and constitutional government instead of absolute rule; freedom of public worship, under whatever form the Churches may determine; a religious toleration always tending to entire religious equality in the eye of the law; the abatement of controversy, the friendly recognition of denominational and doctrinal differences; the federation of Churches, with various disciplines, into a Catholic fellowship, where all are free and all are brotherly—this new state of England, which lies before us to be completed in the twentieth century, is no chance issue. It has come about by the determination of each of the three great sections of English Protestants — Anglicans, Puritans, and Separatists—to be faithful to its own ideal, to establish itself in the common land.

IV

The truth underlying Archbishop Sandys's sentence, about the "small private church" and the "learned Christian kingdom," is this: a Church in a nation like England must share in the national life; it cannot pursue an abstract ideal, it is conditioned in all its movement by the traditions, the habits, and the needs of the commonwealth. It would be a great mistake to suppose that the Separatists were ignorant of this. Barrowe was a man trained in the principles of English law; he sought no liberty for Churches, which was, in his view, inconsistent with the constitution. Henry Jacob had the temperament and the sober speculative habit of the jurist. John Robinson had something of the statesman's outlook; his advice as to the civil government of the new colony, which was followed by the *Mayflower* Compact, was also in the spirit of English history. The fact which Sandys overlooked was that England was undergoing a political change, the influence of which was reflected in the discussions on ecclesiastical polity. It was the eve of democratic constitutionalism. The feudal system was dead, the population was gathering into towns; municipal life—and Congregationalism is municipal freedom in Church government—had begun. The power of the barons, once the protection and then the burden of the people, which had been weakened by the Wars of the Roses, was finally

broken by the Tudor monarchs. The contest
between absolute monarchy and the self-government of the people was at hand. Elizabeth
was the last of the Tudor monarchs; the futility
of the Scottish Stuarts made the triumph of
democracy certain, but a long struggle between the Crown and the people was inevitable. The Separatists were the men who
were looking and labouring for the morrow;
Sandys and his party were facing the setting
sun; Cartwright and those with him thought
for the morrow, but they worked in the spirit
of the past. An eminent Swiss jurisprudent,
M. Borgeaud, does not hesitate to affirm that
the Separatists were the earliest Christian
democrats; he traces the history of modern
democracy to the compact signed in the cabin
of the *Mayflower*. Barrowe may have suspected something of this sort; Henry Jacob
knew it. The wide-reaching issues of their
testimony were not, of course, before them;
but they were watchers by the cradle of the
new England, and they loved the child. They
"builded better than they knew," but they
understood architecture. Truth is one; no
man can be faithful to his vision, however small

may be his field of sight, without helping forward every great movement associated with
his own.   It is much for us to be able to say
of our spiritual forefathers that they were men
who—in times of great confusion, when principles were seething and none could wholly
forecast what form crystallisation would assume
—by a divine instinct associated themselves
with a doctrine which has proved so fruitful
and so far-reaching.

LECTURE II

CONGREGATIONALISM BEFORE
ROBERT BROWNE

Fletcher's "History of Independency"—Congregational and Aggregate Independency—Mr. Fletcher's Anti-State-Churchism — Not all Independents theoretical Congregationalists—Congregationalism the Primitive Type of Churches—Lollard Congregations—English Exiles form Independent Congregations on the Continent — "The Troubles in Frankfort"—Rapid Development of Congregational Practice—Congregational Self-government—The Church prior to the Ministry—Discipline—Return of Exiles to England—What the Marian Persecution had done for Congregationalism—The Christian Congregation —The Use of the term Church in the Puritan Controversy —Persecuted Congregation in London—Accession of Elizabeth—Discontinuance and Revival of Separate Congregations—The Church in the Prisons—Elizabeth's Discouragement of Protestantism—"Reformation without Tarrying for Anie"—Robert Browne—Breach between Puritans and Separatists—Characteristic Differences between them— Purity of Fellowship—The Power of the People—Persecution had proved the People trustworthy—The Church-Meeting—Creed and Covenant—Congregationalism in the New Testament.

LECTURE II

CONGREGATIONALISM BEFORE
ROBERT BROWNE

THE Rev. Joseph Fletcher, whose "History of
Independency"[1] has not received the attention
it deserves, draws a distinction between "Congregational Independency" and what he styles
"Aggregate Independency." By Congregational
Independency he means simply the practice in
congregations of managing their own internal
affairs, either by their members directly or by
those whom they have called to office. By
Aggregate Independency he means the recognised freedom of the Church in the aggregate
from outside control. He has in view not only
a practice, but a practice founded on a doctrine
—and the doctrine is that religion, especially
the Christian religion, is a matter of conscience ;

[1] "The History of the Revival and Progress of Independency
in England." By Joseph Fletcher. 4 vols. London : John
Snow & Co., 1848.

and that as conscience can neither be compelled
by power nor converted by favour, the purely
religious action of Churches must not be subject to external authority, either civil or ecclesiastical.   He points out, moreover, that many of
the "rigid Puritans"—that is, the nonconforming members of the Established Church—were
Congregational, or accidental, Independents.

Mr. Fletcher was one of the young Congregationalists who, about the year 1840, were
under the influence of Edward Miall in the
Nonconformist newspaper.   To them the separation of Church and State was a constant
subject of thought; they saw the evils of
establishment or the blessings of disestablish-
ment everywhere.   In his treatment of Robert
Browne and Separatism, he fixes attention on
the denial of the claim of the civil government to regulate the profession of religion.
" With all deference to the judgment of
others,"[1] he says, " we are compelled to regard Robert Browne as the first in this country
to advocate liberty of conscience on the broad
ground of the distinction between matters civil
and religious.   There can be little doubt, also,

[1] Fletcher, vol. iii. pp. 43, 44.

that the early Brownists held the same views as their leader, since they are so referred to in the contemporaneous writings of the day. The Barrowists were in this and some other respects another class of men, as the Separatists in Holland were a third, and the rigid Puritans in England a fourth. All of them, together with the Baptists, were Congregational Independents; but they did not all hold the same views in respect to the scriptural power of the magistrates in matters of religion." Again he says,[1] "It is plain that the assertion which has been made in our day, respecting the incompatibility of Congregational Independency with the civil establishment of religion, is not absolutely true; since the Congregational Independents of this period—1603 to 1616—or some of them, sought that civil oversight and interference, which, in later periods and in other countries, have actually been connected with the system."

This distinction, which Dr. Dexter quotes with approval, is important. It enables us to understand how it was that, while the Separatists were so few and so weak in the reign of

Fletcher, vol. iii. pp. 47, 48.

King James, Cromwell could call around him,
in the next reign, so many Independents that
he changed the destiny of England. It throws
light on the early ecclesiastical history of Massa-
chusetts and Connecticut, the "blue laws," and
the interference with individual religious liberty,
which drove Roger Williams to Rhode Island
as an escape from Congregational rule. It helps
us to grasp the fact, the assertion of which is
so bewildering to many, that the Pilgrim Fathers
in America and the Brownists in England were
not persecutors; and it frees the persecuting
Congregationalists themselves from the charge
of inconsistency in preaching toleration when
they were the weaker party and refusing toleration when they were in power. The early
Independents included a few who were so because they had worked out a harmonious doctrine of the obligations and rights of the
particular Church, and a great many who
simply practised democracy in their own congregations. The former did not persecute; the
latter did. The distinction has also a backward
look; we shall not understand the development
of English Congregationalism out of the Reformation struggle unless we bear it in mind.

I

Congregationalism is the primitive form of Church government, not only in the sense of its being an apostolic form, but also because it is the form to which Church life naturally and inevitably reverts when Christian men and women, finding either civil or ecclesiastical rule intolerable to conscience, come together in societies for mutual edification. The germ of our Congregationalism was in the teaching and conduct of Wyclif. The "poor priests" whom he sent out to preach had not only evangelistic fervour, they had learned from him very broad principles of religious and civil freedom. The disciples whom they won had a strong impulse of fellowship; they were also instructed in the right and duty of gathering together.

It has been abundantly proved that Lollardry was not sporadic; that it was local and abiding. The Rev. W. H. Beckett[1] has given us maps in which there are graphically presented certain districts which, for successive generations,

[1] "The English Reformation of the Sixteenth Century." By W. H. Beckett. London : R.T.S., 1890.

kept up the tradition of Lollardry; for the most part these were the districts in which Puritanism flourished, and where dissent is strong to-day. Still more lately, Mr. G. M. Trevelyan has dealt with the fable that Lollardry ceased to be influential after the great Reformer's death.[1] Not only did Wyclif leave behind him a few sympathisers among the nobles, he had also founded societies among the people. The first preachers were followed by simple, poor men; "no great Lollard divine succeeded Wycliffe." In the Home Counties, in East Anglia, and in Somerset, from 1400 to 1520, there was persecution of the Lollards. "In the neighbourhood of Beccles, on the borders of Norfolk and Suffolk, great congregations were formed, Lollard schools started, and arrangements made with a certain parchment maker for smuggling in the latest heretical tracts from the capital. This was about the time of the accession of Henry the Sixth.[2] All was done without the protection or patronage of any powerful landowner, simply by the

---

[1] "England in the Age of Wycliffe." By George Macaulay Trevelyan. London: Longmans, Green, & Co., 1899.
[2] 1422.

initiative of the middle classes of the district, searching for a religion suitable to themselves." Nearly a century after, in the reign of Henry the Seventh, one of the signs of the times was " an ever-increasing number of men burnt for Lollardry."

Facts like these cannot but suggest to the imagination companies of men and women, not straggling audiences, but permanent congregations; and the congregations must have had some sort of discipline, using the word in its beautiful Congregational sense, of the care which the members of Christ's body have one for another. A common accusation brought against them was that of Separatism, although the word had not yet come into vogue. They " despised the sacrament of the altar," refused to come to confession, kept away from the parish churches. They are spoken of as " congregations " and " a sect."

II

In the reign of Henry VIII., when religious Reformation was hoped for, and in the reign of Edward VI., when it was advanced, the

D

tendency to this inchoate Congregationalism
was checked; but it received a powerful impulse from the persecutions under Mary Tudor.
Bands of Protestants exiled themselves; they
formed congregations "in sundry places of Germany and Helvetia." There were some also
in Holland. They recognised each other as
independent societies; they spoke of their
assemblies as churches; they were so described
by Archbishop Grindal. The congregations
were self-governed; they had consultations
with each other by letters and messengers, pro-
fiting by one another's experience; but they
recognised no authority, even in great leaders
like Calvin and Beza, to determine their
decisions.

The inevitable drift of such companies into
Congregational Independency is illustrated by
"The History of that Stir and Strife, which was
in the English Church at Frankfort, from the
13th Day of January, Ann. Dom. 1557, forward."

After John Knox had been sent away from
that Church and Mr. Horne chosen their pastor,
a difference arose between him and Mr. Ashley,
one of the members. The elders took up the
case, affirming that Mr. Ashley had, in the

controversy, spoken words injurious to them
all. He denied it, and was summoned to
appear before them and answer for his fault.
The Church was assembled to hear the trial,
when he, not unnaturally for an Englishman,
demanded an impartial tribunal. He said that
"he would not answer before them as competent judges of the cause," seeing "they
shewed themselves an adversary part to him;"
but he would refer the cause for trial to the
whole Church. The pastor threatened him with
an appeal to the magistrates. Ashley "then
handled his own cause in his own name before
the pastor and elders," and offered to submit
the whole matter to eight or ten competent
and impartial men. When the pastor and
elders refused this suggestion, under the plea
that they had received their authority from
the Church, and meant to exercise it, Ashley
appealed to the congregation, and the members
took the matter up.

To shew his displeasure, the offended pastor
declined to exercise his ministry among them.
The members would not excuse his absence; they
summoned him to preach and to come to their
meetings. He would not, and they deposed

him; the elders, who sided with the pastor, were deposed with him. The Church, being now without officers, met and took steps to elect others; whereupon Mr. Horne claimed to be still pastor. But it was too late, neither he nor the elders were able to recover their position.

The members went further. Having found that their order and discipline did not provide for a case like this, where the pastor and elders constituted one side in a controversy and a member of the Church another, they undertook the work of amending their constitution, and produced a new order and discipline—an elaborate document of seventy-three items, in which the freedom of the Church is safeguarded against an unreasonable set of rulers. The pastor and elders had, at the first, appealed to the magistrates, who interfered, although unwillingly, in the interest of the peace of the city. Practically the magistrates sided with the Church; they directed the community to amend its constitution. The heading of the new constitution looks like a note of triumph on the part of the people: " Now followeth the Discipline reform'd and con-

firm'd by the authority of the Church and
Magistrates."

When we remember that these events
happened in 1557–58, twenty-five years before
the publication of Robert Browne's "booke
which sheweth the life and manners of all
true Christians, and how unlike they are unto
Turkes and Papistes and Heathen folke," we
are struck with the somewhat advanced Congregationalism in Frankfort. The document
not only affirms the right of the Church to
elect its officers — Cartwright, as a Puritan,
affirms the same—it declares that the authority
of the Church is prior to that of the ministers,
and that the ministers are subject to the discipline of the Church. In case some of the
ministers and elders are excepted against by
a member or members of the Church, those
excepted against are to have no part in trying
the case; they must stand aside, and the
Church is to nominate substitutes for them on
the judicial body. "If all the ministers and
Seniors be suspected or found Parties, or if
any appeal be made from them; that then
such appeal be made to the body of the congregation, the ministers, Seniors, and Parties

excepted. And that the Body of the Congregation may appoint so many of the Congregation to hear and determine the said matter or matters, as it shall seem good to the Congregation." "The Congregation is to be called or assembled, for causes and at times as shall seem expedient to the ministers and elders; but if they refuse to act, when desired, then the Congregation may itself come together, and that which they, or the major part of them shall judge or decree, shall be a lawful decree and ordinance, of sufficient force to bind the whole Congregation, and every member of the same." They anticipate John Robinson's advice to the Plymouth people, to have more ministers than one; and they declare that neither of them shall be superior in standing or authority to the other. Their definition of a visible Church includes: "(1) Pure and godly doctrine; (2) the right ministration and use of the Sacraments and Common Prayer; (3) honest and godly life, if not in the whole multitude, yet in many of them; (4) discipline, that is, the correction of vices." It is further enacted, that "if any controversy be upon the doubtful meaning of any Word or Words in

the discipline, that first it be refer'd to the
Ministers and Seniors. And if they cannot
agree thereupon, then the thing to be brought
and refer'd to the whole congregation." The
final item provides that "the Discipline and
Orders of the Church shall be read openly
once every Quarter, and warning thereof before
shall be given to the whole Congregation, both
that every member thereof may know his Duty,
and that every man may with liberty quietly
speak his mind, for the changing and amending of it, or any part thereof, according to
God's word; and the same exhibited in writing, with the Arguments and Reasons of that
his Request."

A very significant clause is one concerning discipline. "Altho' this word Discipline
generally doth contain all ecclesiastical Orders
and Ordinances, yet in this place it is properly
taken for the rule of outward honest Orders
and Manners, and of the Punishment and
Correction of Vices." This is a Congregational
note. Discipline, among the Anglicans, meant,
as Robert Browne complained, the power of the
Queen's courts to enforce uniformity. Discipline, as Cartwright and Travers define it,

is mainly the consistorial government of the Church. Discipline here means the care of the whole Church for the purity of life of the members. The execution of discipline is the special charge of six elders, together with the two ministers. "Provided always that the said Ministers and Seniors, severally and jointly, shall have no authority to make any manner of Decrees to bind the Congregation, or any member thereof; but shall execute such Ordinances and Decrees as shall be made by the Congregation, and to them deliver'd."

And yet these men in Frankfort were not true Congregationalists. They were not even "rigid Puritans," for they quote the Apocrypha as if it were Scripture. They are a self-governing community; but it is not because they love the condition, or know that Christ intended His disciples to be such. They are strangers, living their own life in a foreign country, and bringing their common sense to decide domestic details which do not fall under the survey of the law of the land. They accept, and invoke, and plead the general authority of the magistrates; and after all the trouble they have taken with their order and discipline they welcome the time when they shall lay it aside. They had hardly familiarised them-selves with its working when Queen Mary died ; and in the joy of their return to Eng-land, they were willing to accept the order to be provided for them by Parliament. The English congregation at Geneva, which had become cold to them in the former troubles over King Edward's Prayer-Book, now sought their alliance for common work of Reformation in England. These sentences occur in their reply :—

"For our parts, as we have had no conten-tion with you at all aforetime, so we purpose not (as we trust there shall be no cause) to enter into contention with you hereafter. For ceremonies to contend (where it shall be neither in your hands or ours to appoint what they shall be, but in such men's wisdoms as shall be appointed to the devising of the same, and which shall be received by common consent of the Parliament) it shall be to small pur-pose. But we trust that both true Religion shall be restor'd, and that we shall not be burden'd with unprofitable ceremonies. And therefore, as we purpose to submit ourselves

to such Orders as shall be established by
Authority; being not of themselves wicked,
so we would wish you willingly to do the
same. For, whereas all the Reformed Churches
differ among themselves in divers Ceremonies,
and yet agree in the unity of Doctrine, we
see no inconvenience if we use some ceremonies
diverse from them, so that we agree in the
chief points of our Religion; notwithstanding,
if any shall be intruded that shall be offensive,
we, upon just conference and deliberation upon
the same, at our meeting with you in *England*
(which we trust by God's Grace will be shortly)
will brotherly join with you to be suiters for
the reformation and abolishing of the same.
In the mean season, let us with one Heart and
Mind call to the Almighty God, that of His
infinite Mercy He will finish and establish that
Work which He hath begun in our country,
and that we may all lovingly consent together
in the earnest setting forth of His Truth, that
God may be known and exalted, and His
Church perfectly built up thro' Christ our
Lord."

III

A contemporaneous movement of events toward the assertion of Congregational Independency shewed itself in England in a different, but still more effective way—not by internal controversy, the struggle for authority between the ministry and the people, but by fidelity under persecution. The reforming party was impoverished by the self-banishment of so many to the Continent. Their scholars went to the university cities of Germany and Switzerland, taking with them a number of students who formed an important part of the English Churches abroad. Many of their rich people went also, and those self-reliant men who were confident of their ability to earn a living wherever they might be. Of the leaders who remained behind, the most influential were in prison; but the humble, dispirited common people met for worship and encouragement of one another by study of the Scriptures. They were exhorted to continue the practice by letters from the Fleet and King's Bench jails, and such as grew indifferent, justifying their conformity by pleading that though their bodily presence might be in the parish churches their hearts were not there, were severely censured. These small dispersed bodies of the faithful are addressed as the true Church of God in England. Coverdale, editing letters from Bishop Hooper and Archdeacon Philpot, written in their captivity, addresses them to " the congregation," using the precise word which in his New Testament he uniformly employs in translation of the term ἐκκλησία. " A letter sent to the Christian congregation, wherein he (Bishop Hooper) proveth that true faith cannot be kept secret in the heart, without confession thereof openly to the world where occasion serveth." " A letter which he (Master John Philpot) sent to the Christian congregation, exhorting them to refrain themselves from the idolatrous service of the Papists, and to serve God with a pure and undefiled conscience after His Word."

In these inscriptions by Coverdale, as in the story of the Troubles in Frankfort, the use of the words congregation, church, fluctuates between the " Several Church," as it came to be called, and the Protestant Church of England. It is a noteworthy fact, one which may first

strike the sectarian with surprise, that at
the beginning of the Puritan controversy, the
word church was freely used by all parties alike,
of the "particular" or "several" Church—the
Congregational sense; of the Church of England
—the National sense; and the Church Universal—the Catholic sense. A little later, when
the time came for formulating theories of
Church government, a more exclusive use of
the term began. Bancroft, who succeeded
Whitgift in the See of Canterbury, was
startled at the bare Erastianism of his predecessor, and affirmed that there could be no
Church without the divinely ordained Episcopate. Browne and Barrowe had been before
him with the affirmation that there could be
no Church where there was not the discipline
which Christ commanded. And this habit has
come down to our own time. There is scarcely
an Anglican who ever speaks of Congregationalists, Presbyterians, or Methodists, as being
Churches, he calls them "religious societies."
The Independent or Congregational doctrine
was very strict in limiting the word "church"
to two applications—the particular Congregation and the whole body of Christians in

heaven and earth. I have known Congregationalists who have rejoiced in the fact that
they have never committed the fault of calling
the English Establishment a Church. Robinson,
indeed, and others denied that they were so
exclusive, acknowledging that there might be
pure congregations within the Establishment,
and that these were rightly spoken of as
Churches. The Presbyterian habit has been
more generous than that of the Anglicans and
the Congregationalists; they have not refused
to call Churches those organised Christian
fellowships which have not adopted the Presbyterian discipline. And in this they are
faithful to the tradition of the Puritan controversy, which had come down from the days
of the Marian controversy. Archbishop Whitgift wrote frankly of " particular Churches";
Cartwright of " distinct Churches," " particular
Churches," and " the whole Church of England;"
John Robinson of the " parish Churches," [1] and
" the Church of England."

It is not easy to conjecture how many of
these scattered Churches there were under the
persecution. We only know that in different

---

[1] Meaning the congregation, not the building.

parts of England there were some. History has fixed its attention on those in London. Protestants met in the city, in private houses; on the outskirts, in Islington, there were some gravel pits where they assembled. They had regular preaching; they recognised each other as members of a common fellowship. A sentence in George Johnson's "Brief Discourse of Troubles in Amsterdam" (the book in Trinity College Library, Cambridge, from which Dr. Dexter drew his narration of the disagreeable bickering about the pastor's wife and her clothes) throws light on the connection between these London conventicles and the body which afterward became the Southwark Church, the first Congregational Church in England. It refers to the time when the pastor, Francis Johnson, was in prison. "Alderman Tailor's wife, an old professor since Queen Mary's days, having sent him maintenance and help in his imprisonment, said, when she saw his wife's pride, that she would not give any maintenance to maintain pride." The use of the word "professor" here is at once intelligible to old-fashioned Independents; to them a "professor" was a church member.

The assemblies were discontinued on the accession of Elizabeth; they were resumed when it became clear that she did not intend any further reformation, and then they took a more ordered character. There was a Church in the city which had a minister, and observed the Communion of the Lord's Supper. When he was taken to prison they chose another, a Scotsman, who had heard of their worship, and joined himself to them. Their deacon, Cuthbert Sympson, was burnt. We read of baptisms and marriages; the order of their service was described by spies, and recorded in depositions as the habit of such assemblies. Then comes the beautiful story of the Church in the prisons, "whereof Mr. Fitz was pastor." It put out a manifesto: "The order of the Privye Churche in London, whiche by the malice of Satan is falselie slandered and evill spoken of"; and a petition to the Queen, in which they say, "According to the saying of the Almighty our God (Matt. xviii. 20), 'wherever two or three are gathered together in my name, there am I,' so we, a poor congregation whom God hath separated from the churches of England and from the mingled and false worshipping therein used, out of the which assemblies the Lord our only Saviour hath called us, and still calleth, saying, come out from among them, and separate yourselves from them, and touch no unclean thing, then will I receive you, and I will be your God, and you shall be my sons and daughters, saith the Lord (Cor. vi. 17, 18). So as God giveth us strength at this day, we do serve the Lord every Sabbath day in houses, and on the fourth day in the week we meet or come together weekly to use prayer and exercise discipline on them which do deserve it, by the strength and sure warrant of the Lord's good word, as in Matt. xviii. 15–18 (1 Cor. v.)."

The persecution of Separatists under Elizabeth was not so bloody as that of Protestants under Mary; but it was equally relentless, and perhaps even more searching. An extract from the examination of a prisoner, chosen to be interrogated because he was so venerable an old man, shews why these people thought themselves compelled to form churches of their own, and how they associated themselves with the sufferers of the preceding reign. "So long as we might have the word freely preached

E

and the sacraments administered without the preferring of idolatrous gear about it, we never assembled together in houses. But when it came to this point, that all our preachers were displaced by your law, that would not subscribe to your apparel and your law, so that we could not hear none of them in any church by the space of seven or eight weeks, except Father Coverdale, of whom we have a good opinion, and yet (God knoweth) the man was so fearful that he durst not be known unto us where he preached, though we sought it at his house; and then we were troubled and commanded to your courts day by day for not coming to our parish churches. Then we bethought us what were best to do; and we remembered that there was a congregation of us in this city in Queen Mary's days, and a congregation at Geneva, which used a book and order of preaching, ministering of the sacraments and discipline, most agreeable to the word of God, which book is allowed by that godly and well - learned man, Master Calvin, and the preachers there, which book and order we now hold."

John Penry goes further. He shews us the

troubled Puritans looking back on the days of
Mary, and thinking that her open and sanguin-
ary hostility to Protestantism, under any guise,
was better than Elizabeth's purpose of saving
the national Church by the sacrifice of what
the Church, in their opinion, lived for.   One
of the bits of evidence on which he was con-
victed and hanged was the draft of a petition
to the Queen, which was found in his house,
penned in heat as something which he would
like to present to her with his own hand.   Here
are one or two extracts : " If we had had Queen
Mary's days, I think we should have had as
flourishing a church this day as ever any ; for
it is well known that there was then in London,
under the burden, and elsewhere in exile, more
flourishing churches than any now tolerated by
your authority. . . . Thus much we must needs
say, that, in all likelihood, if the days of your
sister Queen Mary, and her persecution, had
continued unto this day, that the Church of
God in England had been far more flourishing
than at this day it is : for then, madam, the
Church of God within this land and elsewhere,
being strangers, enjoyed the ordinances of God's
holy word as far as then they saw.

"But since your majesty came unto your crown we have had whole Christ Jesus, God and man, but we must serve him only in heart.

"And if those days had continued to this time, and those lights risen therein which by the mercy of God have since shined in England, it is not to be doubted but the Church of England, even in England, had far surpassed all the Reformed Churches in the world."

"Then, madam, any of our brethren durst not have been seen within the tents of Antichrist; now they are ready to defend them to be the Lord's, and that he has no other tabernacle upon earth but them."

IV

These quotations indicate the strain under which zealous reformers were labouring in the days of Queen Elizabeth. In the light of them we understand the significance of the title to one of the parts of Robert Browne's book, published in 1582 : "A Treatise of Reformation without tarrying for anie, and of the wickedness of those Preachers, which will not reforme themselves and their charge, because they will tarie till the Magistrate commaunde and compell them."

Let me frankly confess—I do not like Robert Browne; I have not the confidence in him expressed by Dr. Dexter and Dr. Dale. He was a man offensive to his opponents and objectionable to his friends; he betrayed the causes to which he attached himself; and I do not wonder at the heat with which English dissenters have always repudiated the nickname "Brownists." But he was a clear and resolute thinker; he gave himself to study the problems of his time in the simple light of the New Testament, and he produced an admirable and complete doctrine of the Church, which at once determined the whole future of Congregationalism.

He was not so thorough an opponent of the action of the State in religion as Mr. Fletcher takes him to have been. He makes a singular statement to the effect that the magistrate has no right to degrade a faithful minister, but that he has the right to promote him, on the ground that the State ought to advance good men. It was as difficult for him as it is for us to discriminate between the personal influence which a man in office may properly use for the advancement of religion and that official action which ought not to be put forth in Church matters. But he was a strenuous advocate of the duty of Christian believers to form themselves into societies, which the State should not interfere with. I say "the duty," not "the right." Of course the duty involves the right; but it is of some importance which of the two words men are in the habit of using. "There is a substantial identity between the first Separatists and the Congregationalists of to-day; but there is a difference in the proportion given to different aspects of the truth held by them in common and the tone and temper of their testimony. Where we speak of the right of separation they speak of the duty of separation. When we would assert the sanction of Scripture for our polity, we commonly appeal to the words of Christ, ' Where two or three are gathered together in My name, there am I in the midst of them.' The text is occasionally met with in the early Separatist literature; but far more commonly we have the precept, ' Come ye out from among them, and be ye

separate, and touch not the unclean thing.'
It recurs again and again, as if it was exerting
the most solemn constraint upon their conscience; and equally solemn is their continuation of the quotation, 'And I will be a
Father unto you, and ye shall be my sons
and daughters, saith the Lord Almighty;' as
if the Fatherhood and the Sonship—words so
lightly uttered—could only be realised after
the duty of separation had been fulfilled. The
very name 'Separatist,' given them as a nickname, but not repudiated by them, assumed
rather as a badge of their fidelity, shews
how often this passage of Scripture was on
their lips."

With the circulation of Browne's book came a
breach, which proved final, between the Puritans and the Separatists. Henceforth Cartwright had to meet two sets of opponents :
his old antagonists, against whom he had to
justify his nonconformity ; his former associates,
who challenged the consistency, even the recti-
tude, of his continuing in a Church the laws of
which he could not obey. The contest between
the Puritans and the Separatists was just as
uncompromising, though not quite so con-

stant, as that between them both and the
Anglicans.   There could be no harmony between men who thought it was the most urgent
Christian duty to come out of the national
Church and men who thought they were bound
by their allegiance to Christ to keep in.   In
the course of the discussion three points appeared in which Puritanism and Separatism
were hopelessly at variance.

(1.) The Separatists made much of purity of
fellowship, and tried to secure it by looking
to the personal character, as well as to the
soundness of belief, of the members.   It may
seem strange to-day, when all the evangelical
Churches insist that church members should
be living members of the body of Christ, that
the Puritans should have spoken against this.
Two reasons, among others, appear prominently.
Their learning in Church history misled them;
they had the Catholic dread of Donatism.   You
could put the stiffest Puritan to confusion by
calling him a Donatist.   That is a significant
clause in the definition of the Church in the
new Frankfort constitution : " Honest and godly
life, if not in the whole multitude, yet in

many of them ; " and it has plenty of parallels.
At an earlier period in the story, when there
was a discussion whether the congregation
should adopt the Anglican ceremonies or follow
the example of Geneva, the question was put
—*à propos* of schism—" whether the Donatists
were schismatics ? " " Yes," saith Wittingham,
" and also Hereticks, but you are deceiv'd, if
you think that they separated themselves for
ceremonies." Wittingham was a prominent
member of the Puritan section ; but he was
in haste to repel the charge of Donatism.[1]
The other reason was the Puritan's dread of the
Anabaptists, and his sense of obligation to the
national Church. When the first English presbytery, that of Wandsworth, was erected, some
of the parties to it were sent to Newgate. After
an explanation of their design to the chaplain
of the archbishop, who visited them in prison,
they said, " We are not for an unspotted church
on earth, and, therefore, though the Church
of England has many faults, we would not
willingly leave it." To the Separatists it was

[1] John Wesley defended himself from the charge of schism on
precisely the same ground : that he had not departed from the
doctrine, but in some respects from the discipline of the Church.

matter of first moment to seek that the
Churches on earth should be unspotted. They
knew that their judgment was not infallible,
but they could exercise common sense. The
distinction between the visible and the invisible Church, made much of by the Puritans,
was repudiated by them; they believed that
Christian character was patent, and that it
was the one thing essential to a true fellowship. The history of Congregationalism has
confirmed their opinion in this matter; purity
of fellowship remains the first demand of our
Churches.

(2.) The next point of difference between
Puritans and Separatists is concerned with the
place of the people — the members — in the
government and discipline of the Church.
The Church, says Jacob, is a certain democracy—that is its political character, although
Jacob strongly affirms that, on its spiritual
side, it is a monarchy, Christ being the King;
and is an aristocracy of character. Presbyterianism has been proved to be consistent
with democracy; modern Presbyterianism may
be described as an ordered representative demo-

cracy. The tendency in Puritanism to become this was apprehended at once by the Anglican party. "He seeth little," writes Bishop Sandys to Lord Burghley, "who does not perceive that their whole proceedings tend to a mere popularity," *i.e.* popular government. "In the platform set down by these new builders we evidently see the spoliation of the patrimony of Christ, and a popular state to be sought," write Sandys and Grindal to another prelate. But Cartwright was as great a foe to "popularity" as the bishops themselves; the people are to elect their ministers and leave administration to them.

The Separatists called the members individually to take part in the government of the Church, and this was not a mere demand of consistency in the working out of their doctrine; nor was it a bit of policy, a determination to commit the people as deeply as possible to the cause. It was the result of experience also. The fidelity of the people had been tried in times of persecution, and it was at least equal to that of their leaders. The number of recantations, either final or temporary, is one of the most pathetic features in the story of the English martyrdoms; it lends great interest to that first chapter of the second volume of Mr. Froude's "History of England," perhaps the most beautiful chapter in the book. He refers us to Latimer's account of Bilney as a typical narrative. "I knew a man myself," says the great preacher, "Bilney, little Bilney, that blessed martyr of God, what time he had borne his fagot, and was come again to Cambridge, had such conflicts within himself, beholding the image of death, that his friends were afraid to let him be alone; they were fain to be with him day and night, and comforted him as they could, but no comforts would serve. As for the comfortable places of Scripture, to bring them unto him, it was as though a man would run him through the heart with a sword; yet afterward, for all this, he was revived, and took his death patiently, and died well against the tyrannical See of Rome." Mr. Trevelyan gives us the same picture. There are so many recantations; even John Purvey, the valorous fellow-worker with Wyclif, when the slaughter began, recanted; as did Cranmer when the last fires were burning out. The humbler people were more faithful than their leaders; not recantation, but fidelity, marks the story of the peasant and the working woman. We may account for this fact, may plead the influence of culture on the development of nerves, and the large-mindedness which suggests doubt; but the fact remains — the Christian commonalty had shewn itself worthy to be trusted. John Robinson's noble scorn of those who contemptuously upbraided God's people with inconstancy, instability, pride, contention, and such like evils, nicknaming them Symon the saddler, Tomkin the tailor, Billy the bellows-mender, has a historical justification in the part the people had taken in the Reformation.

Equally has experience warranted the Separatists' confidence in the ability of pure churches to maintain a lofty ideal of fellowship and mutual edification. Robinson's testimony to the character of the church meetings in Leyden is well known. "If ever I saw the beauty of Zion, and the glory of the Lord filling His tabernacle, it hath been in the manifestation of the divers graces of God in the Church, in that heavenly harmony and comely order wherein, by the grace of God, we are set and walk." Henry Barrowe—courtier, law student, man of the world—said the same thing of the 'Church in London. "The solitary and contemplative life," said Lancelot Andrews to him when he was in jail, "I hold the most blessed life. It is the life I would choose." Barrowe's reply shows something of the inner life of the Church for whose sake he was suffering. "You speak philosophically, but not Christianly. So sweet is the harmony of God's graces unto me in the congregation and the conversation of the saints at all times, as I think myself as a sparrow on the housetop when I am exiled from them." From that time to our own the most cultivated and saintly leaders in Congregationalism have shewn the same appreciation of the church meeting. It would be easy to make a catena of utterances to this effect, not from controversial writings or sermons, but from hymns, and letters, and biographical memoirs, ending with Dr. Dale's lofty description of its sanctity in his address to a joint meeting of the Baptist and Congregational Unions in 1886. "To be at a church meeting—apart from any prayer that is offered, any hymn that is sung, any words that are spoken—is for me one of the

chief means of grace. To know that I am sur-
rounded by men and women who dwell in God,
who have received the Holy Ghost, with whom
I am to share the eternal righteousness and
eternal rapture of the great life to come, this
is blessedness. I breathe a Divine air. I am
in the new Jerusalem, which has come down
out of heaven from God, and the nations of the
saved are walking its streets of gold. I rejoice
in the joy of Christ over those whom He has
delivered from eternal death and lifted into the
light and glory of God. The Kingdom of Heaven
is there."

(3.) The third point of difference between the
Separatists and the Puritans is the confidence
of the Puritans that it was possible for them to
give adequate expression to the truth of God
in creeds and confessions, while the Separatists
affirmed that all creeds and confessions were
partial and temporary utterances, for that the
Lord had more light yet to break forth out of
His holy word. Their church covenants bound
the members to hold all God's truth already
revealed or yet to be revealed. So deeply was
this thought, that there is no finality in doc-

trine, rooted in their faith, that the *May-flower* Compact applies it to political principles. The signers of that document bound themselves to no constitution already adopted, but "to enact, constitute, and frame such just and equall lawes, ordinances, acts, constitutions, and offices, from time to time, as shall be thought most meete and good for the generall good of the Colonie, unto which we promise all due submission and obedience." The growth of toleration followed from the adoption of this principle. Again and again the limited tolera-tion of the Independents has been pointed out; it was for Christians, Protestant Christians only. They had not solved—we have not yet solved—the problem of tolerating all religious beliefs in a community, when such toleration would pro-bably result in an attempt, by some of the sects tolerated, religiously to upset the order of civil government. Their claim to be consistent lovers of religious liberty does not lie in their success-ful grappling with this difficulty; although English Congregationalists have been always advocates of the largest liberty the Government has been ready to grant, and have urged a full application of the method of freedom. It lies in their tenacious, courageous acknowledgment that never yet has so much enlightenment been granted to the interpreters of God's revealed will, that they could say, "We know not in part, but perfectly."

I referred in my former Lecture to the fact that the Separatists were living in the last hours of Absolutism in Church and State, on the eve of English democracy. Many interesting discussions have been going on as to the causes of this democratic movement, and the conditions under which it became inevitable. The Teutonic home, and the traditions of the German agricultural life; trade guilds and the growth of large towns; the free municipalities of Holland and the intercourse between Dutch and English manufacturers; the influence of the Renascence and the printing-press — all have been brought in to illustrate a fact which summed up in itself all that these forces had to give. Such considerations shew us what made it possible for Congregational Churches to be, but they do not account for Congregationalism. It is always to the Bible the Separatists turn when they would defend their ecclesiastical faith. It is no wonder that such men found Congregationalism in the New Testament; the wonder would have been had they found anything else.

LECTURE III

PRESBYTERIANS AND INDEPENDENTS

Dr. Shaw's "Church of the Commonwealth" — The Church of England a Presbyterian Church—The short Duration of this Establishment—English Presbyterianism prejudiced by its History—The Scottish Committee and the Westminster Assembly—The Scottish Army and the Scottish Arguments—A rigid Presbyterianism rejected by the English People—Baxter's Testimony—The Voluntary Associations — Adam Martindale — Independents in the Westminster Assembly — Declaration of Liberty of Conscience—What it meant—Independents' Scheme of Toleration — Fails from Over-Definition — Baxter and the Fundamentals — Independents' Zeal for Orthodoxy—Projects for Union between Presbyterians and Independents—"The Happy Union"—The Crispian Controversy — The Salters' Hall Split—Unitarianism — Evangelical Presbyterians become Congregationalists—Defoe Memorial Church—Relation of Separatists to Independents.

LECTURE III

PRESBYTERIANS AND INDEPENDENTS

A VALUABLE addition has been made to the story of the struggle between Presbyterianism and Independency in England by the publication of Dr. Shaw's "History of the English Church during the Civil Wars and under the Commonwealth." [1] He had previously edited the Minutes of the Manchester Classis, 1646–60, and the Minutes of the Bury Classis, 1647–57, and had demonstrated how systematically it had been attempted to work the Presbyterian government in Lancashire. In his later book he has shewn that the system was more widely prevalent than we have been in the habit of thinking. The very title is significant. "The English Church," as the Parliament established it in 1648, and as Cromwell administered it, was a Presbyterian Church. The Scottish Commissioners had succeeded in

[1] London : Longmans, Green & Co., 1900.

forcing through the Westminster Assembly a complete scheme of consistorial rule—Congregational Presbyteries, that is the English name for Kirk Sessions ; Classes, the English name for Presbyteries ; Provincial Synods ; and a National Assembly—the orders ranging one above another, in ecclesiastical authority as well as in dignity. This system was adopted after debate, and promulgated by Acts of Parliament, exactly as the present Episcopal Church was established.

Here are some words from Dr. Shaw's preface : " The years 1640–60 witnessed the most complete and drastic revolution which the Church of England has ever undergone. Its whole structure was ruthlessly demolished— Episcopacy, the Spiritual Courts, Deans and Chapters, Convocation, the Book of Common Prayer, the Thirty-nine Articles, and the Psalter. . . . On the clean - swept ground an entirely novel church system was erected. In place of Episcopal Church government a Presbyterian organisation was introduced, and a Presbyterian system of ordination. For the Spiritual Courts were substituted Presbyterian Assemblies (Parochial, Classical, and Provin-

cial), acting with a very real censorial jurisdiction, but in final subordination to a Parliamentary Committee sitting at Westminster.
Instead of the Thirty-nine Articles the Confession of Faith was introduced, and the Direc-
tory in place of the Book of Common Prayer.
New catechisms and a new metrical version
were prepared, a parochial survey of the whole
country was carried out, and extensive re-
organisation of parishes effected." "There is
hardly a parallel in history to such a constitutional revolution as this."

It was, however, only a paper revolution.
The Long Parliament was not the nation; it
would not have been the Long Parliament
had its leaders thought that they had the
judgment of the people with them. Nor did
the Westminster Assembly represent the religious spirit and convictions of England. Not
more than half the counties even professed
to adopt the classical system; where it was
adopted it was only indifferently observed. In
the few cases, as in Lancashire, where the
classis met regularly, there was opposition to
it both from ministers and Churches. It is
very improbable that it would have become

effective in time, and time was not given. Twelve years after its passing through Parliament came the Restoration, and the re-establishment of Episcopacy. In 1662 there was a new Act of Uniformity, and about two thousand Puritan clergymen, most of them styled Presbyterian, were ejected from their livings. In 1688, when William III. began his rule of fourteen years, the hope of the Presbyterians partially revived. Now they would have been content with far less than a National Presbyterian Church; they did, however, expect that the Church of England would have been made broad enough to take them in. A Bill of Comprehension was laid before Parliament with that object. It passed the House of Lords, but was rejected by the Commons. In the following year "the Toleration Act" was passed; it was a statute "for exempting Protestant subjects dissenting from the Church of England from the penalties of certain laws." The Presbyterians, with other Nonconformists, were allowed liberty of public worship and self-government; but they were declared dissenters, not members of the Church of England. From that time

Presbyterianism steadily declined. In the eighteenth century most Evangelical Presbyterian churches became Congregational ; a portion of the Unitarian denomination preserving the tradition of the old system, but loosely administering it, is what now remains of the Classical Church of the Commonwealth.

I

English Presbyterianism was prejudiced at the first, and ultimately was ruined by the very circumstances which alone made its adoption possible. It was born in the throes of revolution. It was a Church of safety—to borrow the language of revolutionary times. The Long Parliament had become a mere " Committee of Safety," and the establishment of a Presbyterian Church was one of its necessities. In the struggle between the Parliamentary forces and the army of Charles I. an alliance with Scotland seemed essential, and the only terms on which the Scots would grant their help were the adoption by England of the Solemn League and Covenant, and the establishment of the National Church after the rigid Presbyterian

model. To a religious mind the story of the
Westminster Assembly is painful reading—the
contrast is so great between the dignity, the
solemn severity, the large and lofty reach of the
Confession of Faith, and the subtlety and dis-
ingenuousness which marked the ecclesiastical
discussions. A political league with Scotland
was desired, the religious covenant was un-
welcome. Engagements of this sort are uncon-
genial to the English temper; the more sacred
their terms, the more the Englishman shrinks
from them. But dogmatic confidence and
political necessity are both purblind and ruthless; the covenant, with its solemn adjuration
of Father, Son, and Holy Ghost, had to be
taken. Attempts to reconcile the demands of
the Presbyterian majority and the scruples of
the Independents were thwarted by the Scottish Commissioners, some of whom took small
part in the discussions of the Assembly, but
ceaselessly acted on it through its Scottish
debaters. Here is an extract from Baillie. He
is reporting a discussion on the ruling eldership,
in which the main body were opposed by the
Independents. " When all were tired, it came
to the question. There was no doubt but we

would have carried it by far most voices; yet because the opposite were men verie considerable, above all gracious and learned little Palmer, we agreed upon a committee to satisfie if it were possible the dissenters. For this end we meet to-day, and I hope ere all be done we shall agree. All of them were ever willing to admitt elders in a prudentiall way; but this to us seemed a most dangerous and unhappie way, and therefore was peremptorily rejected. We trust to carry at last, with the contentment of sundry once opposite, and silence of all, their divine and scriptural institution. This is a point of high consequence, and upon no other we expect so great difficultie, except alone on Independencie, wherewith we purpose not to medle in haste till it please God to advance our armie, which we expect will much assist our arguments."

We are not to read his words as a suggestion that the Scottish troops are to come to London and train their guns on the Jerusalem Chamber. It is not the army, but the advancement of the army, which Baillie looks to to assist the arguments. In the early days of the Civil War, while Cromwell's series of brilliant victories was not dreamed of, a demonstration that the issue of the struggle depended on the Scottish army would facilitate a Presbyterian triumph in the Assembly. When the Scottish troops gained a victory, the Presbyterians were domineering; when the Parliamentarian forces were successful, the Independents became exacting. However conciliatory the Presbyterians might occasionally be, the Scottish Commissioners were always biding their time to reassert themselves. At last they carried their points, but the Assembly had long ceased to have moral weight. An enduring Church could not be established in such times, and by such men.

Another difficulty appeared when the attempt was made to settle Presbyterianism in the parishes and counties—the Churches would not have it. There were not approving clergymen enough in most districts to work the polity, nor men fit to be ordained. Dr. Shaw says broadly, but correctly, that "the Presbyterianism of the Civil War was an abrupt and startling and illogical expansion from the basis of English Puritanism." [1] He quotes Baxter, not as uniformly accurate in his estimate of facts, but as

[1] Shaw, vol. i. p. 6.

right in tone. " Though Presbytery generally
took in Scotland, yet it was but a stranger
here, and it found some ministers that lived in
conformity to the bishops' liturgies and ceremonies (however much they might wish for
reformation), and the most that quickly after
were ordained were but young students in the
universities at the time of the change of church
government, and had never well studied the
points on either side; and though most of the
ministers then in England saw nothing in the
Presbyterian way which they could not cheer-
fully concur in, yet it was but few that had
resolved on their principles. And when I came
to try it, I found that most that ever I could
meet with were against the *jus divinum* of lay
elders, and for the moderate primitive Episcopacy, and for a narrow Congregational or
parochial extent of ordinary churches, and for
an accommodation of all parties in order to
concord." Baxter's words are very significant.
The English people are practically, not academically, minded; it is at once their strength and
their weakness. In Parliament, in town councils, in religious committees, and business meetings, you close a discussion by pronouncing it

academic. The advocates of the Puritan discipline in the times of Elizabeth were academics
— like Cartwright, the Cambridge vice-
chancellor, and Travers, the preacher at the
Temple; so were the Presbyterian leaders in
the Westminster Assembly. Their scheme was
very complete, and it was authoritatively issued,
but the parish clergy, with their working
experience, would not have it.

II

The parish clergy were not content with
disregarding the system; within five years
another system, essentially Congregational, was
adopted in many parts of the country—adopted,
too, where the Puritan tradition was strong.
This was Baxter's scheme of Voluntary Associations, which he expounded with his usual
copiousness and clearness. These associations
repudiated the right of commanding the attendance of ministers within their bounds; they
made no claim to authority, they exercised
only advisory influence over the particular
churches.

This scheme is fully described by Baxter, its

author. An extract from Adam Martindale's autobiography will show how it appeared to an ordinary country parson.[1] " In September 1653, at a meeting of ministers at Wilmeslow, the 14th day of that month, a motion was made, and a letter drawne to invite many other ministers to give them the meeting at Knutsford on the 20th of October, being the exercise day, as accordingly many did; and there they agreed upon a voluntary association of themselves and their churches, if it could be done, for mutuall advice and strengthening each other. Into this societie I quickly after fell, and met with much comfort and assistance; but by this meanes our worke was encreased by meeting frequently about classicall businesse, and preaching in our turnes a lecture when we so met.

" If it be asked how I got satisfaction to act with them now, when I had scrupled some things concerning classicall government at the time of my being at Gorton, I answer, the case was not the same. Here was only a voluntary association of such as were desirous to advise and assist one another, nor did we

[1] " Adam Martindale's Diary, ' Chetham Society, p. 112.

look upon ourselves as having any pastorall inspection over one another's congregations; but onely to be helpfull to them in a charitable way : we pretended not to any power to convent any before us, or suppresse any minister because dwelling in such a place, within such a verge, and differing from us in practice."

Martindale was not a Congregationalist; he was a parish clergyman of the Puritan type. He disliked the Separatists as cordially as did Baxter, and complains of the intrusion of Independents from Manchester when he was at Gorton, and from Bowdon into his country charge at Rostherne. It is the true English spirit which asserts itself in him; the determination to have municipal freedom, and a dread of clerical courts. An Episcopal system is not un-English, neither is Congregational Independency; Presbyterianism of the Continental and Scottish character is.

III

The struggle between a voluntary Presbyterianism, adopted as a "prudential" system, dependent on the free consent of the particular

Churches, and Presbyterianism claiming the *jus divinum*, demanding to be established by Parliament as an authoritative and uniform system over every congregation in the land, was in reality the great conflict of the Westminster Assembly. A conciliatory temper often appeared in both parties, notwithstanding the trust in the Scottish army of the Presbyterians, and the dependence of the Independents on Cromwell, and their occasional alliance with the Erastian members of the House of Commons. The opposing parties had very much in common; admiration, even affectionate regard, sprang up between them as they came to know each other in debate. Terms of accommodation were more than once suggested, and were proposed with hope. But when the critical point was reached—authority or free consent, uniformity or liberty of difference among the Churches— the quarrel broke out afresh; the conciliatory temper was lost in mutual exasperation and a deeper distrust. The same fundamental difference appears in the histories of the Assembly, as written by constitutional Congregationalists and constitutional Presbyterians almost down to the present day. It is a conscientious

G

difference; we have here no battle between "frogs and mice," still less a greedy contest between "kites and crows." It is rooted in the dialectic habit, and represents the various temperaments, of men equally honourable, equally religious, equally striving after abiding concord in the faith. Some men are, by natural constitution, lovers of order in the first place; they believe that under good order individual liberty is secure : other men attach the supreme importance to freedom, and trust that free men, free societies, will work out order. The fight in the Assembly ended in the triumph of uniformity, but liberty has ultimately prevailed. The history of England subsequently has, however, made it evident that the strife will be perpetual so long as there is a Church established by, and acting with the authority of, the State.

As part of this struggle there arose that great historic incident, which stirs in Englishmen the same deep, impassioned reverence which Americans feel when any allusion is made to the voyage of the *Mayflower*—the plea for liberty of conscience advanced by Thomas Goodwin, Philip Nye, Jeremiah Burroughs, William Bridge, and Sidrach Simson. A striking picture found in many a Congregational home has impressed this plea for liberty of conscience in the Westminster Assembly on the national memory. No single incident occurred like that which is here pourtrayed, but the picture is true to the spirit of the Independents in the Assembly. Historians have pointed out that the doctrine of toleration as advanced by these men, was not the modern doctrine ; it was much more limited, it was not based on the universal right, the inevitable necessity, of liberty of thought, which is generally accepted to-day. Mr. Hunter says that Locke and Chillingworth, not the five dissenting brethren, were the fathers of toleration. Dr. Hetherington, a Presbyterian historian of the Assembly, points out that the Independents did not give unlimited toleration when they had the power. And Dr. Shaw dwells on the fact that what was pleaded for was not a universal regard for tender consciences, but freedom for their own Congregational action under the Church which was to be established. All this is true, and I do not know that the five brethren are to be censured for confining their protest to the matters under discussion, without encumbering themselves with large generalisations, which only an experience very much broader and more specific than any which men then possessed would warrant. It has been a weakness, rather than a strength, in modern English Nonconformity, that so many Nonconformists have invoked, on small occasions, great principles, the full application of which they have not had the opportunity of testing. What the five dissenters did was to utter, to utter firmly, their own demand, and refuse to be turned aside when they were told that their action was endangering interests which were as sacred to them as to their opponents. It shows moral courage in an educated man when he does not shrink before the *argumentum ad invidiam*; the possession of such courage, quite as much as large vision, is a qualification for pioneering progressive thought.

Dr. Hetherington criticises the dissenting brethren severely. He writes thus:[1] "What we have termed the political Independents of the army were composed of sectarians of every

---

[1] "History of the Westminster Assembly of Divines," by W. M. Hetherington, D.D., LL.D. Edinburgh: James Gemmell, 1878. P. 149.

shade of opinion; and from them, rather than from the religious Independents in the Assembly, arose the idea of *toleration*, of which so much use was subsequently made. As used by those military sectarians, the meaning of the term was, that any man might freely utter the ravings of his own heated fancy, and endeavour to proselytise others, be his opinions what they might, even though manifestly subversive of all morality, all government, and all revelation. Such a toleration, for instance, as would include alike Antinomians and Anabaptists, though teaching that they were set free from and above the rules of moral duty so completely, that to indulge in the grossest licentiousness was in them no sin; and Levellers and Fifth-Monarchy men, whose tenets went directly to the subversion of every kind of constituted government, and all distinctions in rank and property. This was what *they* meant by *toleration*,—and this was what the Puritans and Presbyterians condemned and wrote against with startled vehemence. And it is neither to the credit of the Independent divines of that period, nor of their subsequent admirers and followers, that they seem to countenance such a toleration, the real meaning of which was civil, moral, and religious anarchy."

I have no quarrel with this general representation of the matter at issue, but I say that, instead of reflecting no credit on the Independent divines, it is a high tribute to their courage and wisdom and composure that when the question of toleration was before the Assembly, in such guise as it here assumes, they did not draw back from their demand. It means much that they stood firm under conditions in presence of which Martin Luther quailed. "Pious, gentle, able, acute, learned" —these are some of the epithets Dr. Hetherington distributes among the group. They knew the odium which an association with Antinomians and Levellers would draw on them; they foresaw the grave questions which would have to be grappled with if a beginning of toleration were made; they perceived the controversial advantage which they were giving to their opponents, and they did not flinch. Dr. Hetherington goes on to admit, "It is, however, true that out of the discussions which this claim of unbounded and licentious toleration raised, there was at length evolved the idea of religious toleration, such as is demanded by man's solemn and dread characteristic of personal responsibility, and consequent inalienable right to liberty of conscience."

That they deliberately faced this issue appears from the following extract from Baillie : " We hope shortelie to gett the Independents put to it to declare themselves either to be for the rest of the Sectaries or against them. If they declare against them they will be but a small inconsiderable companie ; if for them all honest men will cry out upon them for separating from all the Reformed Churches to joyne with Anabaptists and Libertines." They made their choice ; met a subtle, logical dilemma by a demand whose brevity is significant.[1] In the end of November 1645 " Goodwin, Nye, Simson, Bridge, and Burroughs were requested to bring in their desires concerning Church government. On the 4th of December they accordingly presented such their desires :—

" 1. Ordination to be permissibly performed by sufficiently qualified persons in case there be no presbytery.

[1] Shaw, vol. ii. p. 48.

" 2. Their congregations to be exempt from Classical, Provincial, and National Synods in respect of jurisdiction."

" 3. Liberty to form congregations."

IV

The real weakness of the Independent position appeared later on, when, under Cromwell's Protectorate, the Independents were instructed to formulate a scheme of toleration. Cromwell himself was a large-minded man. Personally, he was a strong Calvinist and a sincere Congregationalist; but as charged with care for the national concord, and seeing the peril of continued religious strife, he would have encouraged ministers of conspicuous piety with very different theories of Church government. It was understood that popish and prelatic clergymen were to be excluded; this was on political grounds. Exactly as Barrowe, and Greenwood, and Penry were charged with sedition in Elizabeth's days, and with more reason, Roman Catholics were treated as seeking the political supremacy of the Pope, and Episcopalians as working for the restoration of the Stuarts. The exclusion is inconsistent with a generous doctrine of liberty of conscience; and the mistake seemed to justify the ruthless ejectment of the Puritan clergy when Charles II. came to the throne. But we must consider the national danger; and Cromwell's good faith is apparent in the fact that Episcopalian ministers, who were manifestly devoted to their parishes, and not preaching faction, were continued in their cures. The forbidding of liberty of speech to Atheists, Anti-Trinitarians, and others was a necessary consequence of the fact that the scheme of toleration was proposed in continuation of legislative proposals for a scheme for "the Propagation of the Gospel," which since 1652–53 had been, more or less, before Parliament. It was taken for granted "that the Christian religion, as contained in the Scriptures, be held forth and recommended as the public profession of the nation;" "and the discovery and confutation of error, heresy, and whatever is contrary to sound doctrine," were looked upon as the concern of Parliament equally with "the encouragement and maintenance of able and painful preachers for the instructing of the people." No method of reconciling perfect liberty for all consciences with the existence of a Church, established and sustained by the State, has even yet been discovered, and in those days it was almost universally believed that, without such a national Church, there could be no public profession of the Christian religion. Nor had men then detected the fallacy into which even Dr. Hetherington has stumbled, the assumption, namely, that because some doctrines are subversive of society, to tolerate their utterance is "civil, moral, and religious anarchy." It needed Milton's lofty courage and clarion words—"Let truth and falsehood grapple; who ever knew truth put to the worse, in a free and open encounter?"—to stir the conscience of the nation; and Locke's clear reasoning to convince its judgment that loyalty to truth demands the liberty of open utterance for all opinions which men hold.

In a report presented to a Parliamentary Committee, 18th February 1651, to which twenty-seven names are attached — among them Nye and Simson and Bridge, dissenting brethren of the almost defunct Assembly, and John Owen and John Goodwyn, the great Cal-

vinistic and Arminian divines of the Independents—there are some wise and weighty
recommendations.[1] "It is desired that no
person be required to receive the Sacrament
further than their light shall lead them unto,
so no person sent forth to preach and already
placed, or who shall be placed in any parish
within this nation, be compelled to administer
the Sacraments to any but such as he shall
approve of as fit for the same." "That whereas
divers persons are not satisfied to come to the
public places of hearing the word, upon this
account that these places are dedicated and
consecrated, that the Parliament will be pleased
to declare that such places are made use of
and continued only for the better convenience
of persons meeting together for the public worship of God, and for no other consideration."
"That all persons dissenting to the doctrine
and way of worship owned by the State, or
consenting thereunto, and yet not having the
advantage or opportunity of some of the publick meeting-places, commonly called churches,
be required to meet (if they have any constant
meeting) in places publickly known, and to

[1] Shaw, vol. ii. pp. 82, 83.

give notice unto some magistrate of such their place of ordinary meetings." A later Parliamentary declaration—the historic " Instrument of Government"—declares that[1] "to the public profession (of the Christian religion) held forth, none shall be compelled by penalties or otherwise ; but that endeavours be used to win them by sound doctrine and the example of a good conversation." "That such as profess faith in God by Jesus Christ (though differing in judgment from the doctrine, worship, or discipline publicly held forth) shall not be restrained from, but shall be protected in, the profession of the faith and exercise of their religion ; so as they abuse not this liberty to the civil injury of others and to the actual disturbance of the public peace on their parts ; provided this liberty be not extended to Popery or Prelacy, nor to such as, under the profession of Christ, hold forth and practise licentiousness."

Up to this point all went well ; but on the words "faith in God by Jesus Christ," a discussion arose, the issue of which was that the whole scheme came to nothing. "Considering that such words contained the fundamentals

[1] Shaw, vol. ii. p. 85.

of religious belief, it was proposed that all should have a due measure of liberty who professed the fundamentals ; and a Committee of Divines was nominated to define them." At once the old dogmatic spirit was aroused, and the Independents, by their definitions, began a work of exclusion. " I knew," says Baxter,[1] " how ticklish a business the enumeration of Fundamentals was, and of what very ill consequence it would be if it were ill done, and how unsatisfactorily that question, *What are your Fundamentals?* is usually answered to the Papists." Baxter wisely suggested that they should " distinguish between the *sense* or *matter* and the *words;* and that it's only the *sense* that is primarily and properly our *Fundamentals,* and the *words* no further than as they are needful to express that *sense* to others, or represent it to our own conception." He further proposed that they should substitute for the word *Fundamental* the word *Essential,* which proposal is not exactly an Irenicon ; but another declaration from him is, " that *quoad rem* there is no more *Essential* or *Fundamental* in religion, but what is con-

Reliquiæ Baxterianæ. London, 1696. Pp. 197-99.

tained in our Baptismal Covenant, *I believe in God the Father, Son, and Holy Ghost, and give up myself in covenant to Him, renouncing the Flesh, the World, and the Devil.*" "I would have had the Brethren," he further said, "to have offered the Parliament the *Creed, Lord's Prayer, and Decalogue* alone as our Essentials or Fundamentals, which at least *contain all* that is necessary to salvation, and hath been by all the ancient Churches taken for the sum of their religion. And whereas they still said, *A Socinian or a Papist will subscribe all this*, I answered them, So much the better, and so much the fitter it is to be the matter of our concord. But if you are afraid of communion with *Papists* and *Socinians*, it must not be avoided by making a new Rule or Test of Faith which they will not subscribe to, or by forcing others to subscribe to more than *they* can do, but by calling them to account whenever in preaching or writing they contradict or abuse the truth to which they have subscribed." That last sentence is very characteristic of Baxter, who wrote a hundred and sixty - eight treatises, mostly long and always controversial, and whose perpetual wonder was that one so reasonable as he should have scarcely any to agree with him.

"One merry passage," which Baxter tells us "awakened laughter," will shew the elaboration to which the discussion lengthened. "Mr. Sympson caused them to make this a Fundamental, that *He that alloweth himself or others in any known sin cannot be saved.* I pleaded against the word 'allowed,' and told them that many a thousand lived in wilful sin, which they could not be said to allow themselves in, but confessed it to be sin, and went on against conscience, and yet were impenitent and in a state of death; and that there seemed a little contradiction between known sin and allowed; so far as a man knoweth that he sinneth, he doth not *allow*, that is, approve it. Other exceptions there were, but they would have their way, and my opposition to anything did but heighten their resolution. At last I told them, As stiff as they were in their opinion and way, I would force them with one word to change or blot out all that Fundamental. I urged them to take my wager, and they would not believe me, but marvelled what I meant. I told them that the Parliament took the Independent way of separation to be a sin, and when this Article came before them they would say, By our Brethren's own Judgment we are all damned Men, if we allow the Independents or any other Sectaries in their sin. They gave me no answer, but they left out all that Fundamental."

All this is very noteworthy; it brings into prominence a fact which must be borne in mind if we are to understand the relation of Presbyterians and Independents under the Commonwealth — that the Independents were more jealous for orthodoxy than the Presbyterians. Baxter speaks of "the over-orthodox Doctors, Owen and Cheynell"; and attributes the failure of their scheme of toleration to the fact that "they took it to be their Duty in all those Fundamentals to put in those words which, as they said, did obviate the Heresies and Errors of the Divines." This was the normal attitude of the Independents from Browne and Barrowe down to the first half of the nineteenth century. It was not their universal temper; there always have been men among them—like Peter Sterry in the seventeenth century, Isaac Watts and Philip Doddridge in the eighteenth, and a large majority of them in the nineteenth—who did not confound zeal for orthodoxy with fidelity to the truth; but it was something more than a general attitude, it was normal, sure on critical occasions to appear. It was part of their Separatism; they loved the church fellowship of like-minded men, not only for the gracious discipline of morals it afforded, but equally because it gave them freedom to profess their full-orbed system of truth. It accounts for the contrast between the tepid interest the Independents of the Assembly took in schemes of Accommodation and the heartiness with which they threw themselves into the scheme of Toleration. Accommodation meant the surrender of testimony to some truths, secondary, indeed, but very dear to them, for the sake of more important interests; Toleration meant an equal liberty for them all to form assemblies in which everything they held as Christian truth might be freely uttered. The practice of Church covenanting which marked the Congregationalists of the seventeenth century, and the frequency with which they put out Confessions of Faith, are indications of the same regard for minute and systematic utterances of truth.

H

V

The extreme orthodoxy of the Independents frustrated, in the end of the seventeenth century, what looked like a very promising scheme for uniting them with the Presbyterians in one denomination. For three-fourths of the century they were drawing nearer to each other in confidence and esteem, though they did not always perceive it. In the controversies of the Commonwealth they were learning to know each other; and in the parishes non-controversialists were working side by side with mutual respect. Under the Restoration they were fellow-sufferers: the iniquitous oppression beneath which they groaned bound them in tender sympathy; the anxieties which weighed down the ministers and congregations, who still came together with difficulty and danger, abolished the distinction between them. They joined together to accomplish the Revolution and set William III. on the throne. There is in London a "General Board of the three Denominations"—Baptist, Congregational, and Presbyterian — which still has the right of direct access to the throne for the service they rendered in the political struggles which finally established the monarchy of the House of Hanover. When the Comprehension Bill was lost and the Act of Toleration was passed, and the Episcopal Church was finally established as exclusively the National Church, the only political distinction between Presbyterians and Independents was gone. Their congregations coalesced; their ministers were Congregational or Presbyterian, not because of any difference in the government of the churches, but according to the accidental attachment of the people, in one part of the country or another, to either of the two names. Trust - deeds were drawn, declaring lands and buildings to be held for the use of congregations of Protestant Dissenters of the Presbyterian or Independent denomination, and to this day it is a moot point whether the words signified two denominations, or one denomination with transferable names. It was a state of things which would have been intolerable to the Scottish Presbyterians of the Assembly; it was very delightful to the children of the Puritans, and it seemed to promise an entire union between them.

A project for such a union, known under the name of " the Happy Agreement," or " the Happy Union," was ruined by the extreme Calvinism—so-called, but wrongly so-called— of the Independents. A London minister chose this particular time for republishing some writings of his father, Dr. Tobias Crisp, in which the doctrine of the Atonement was set forth in a very obnoxious form. The writer had been an Arminian ; when he became a Calvinist he rushed into an extreme which it needs a skilful theologian to distinguish from Antinomianism. He went even beyond the Supralapsarians in that he taught that a man was justified before his faith, viz., in the eternal decree by which he was ordained unto eternal life. Dr. Daniel Williams, an eminent Presbyterian—a man now known for the library he left behind him containing books and manuscripts of the greatest use in Puritan history, and for the university scholarships he founded, but then known for the grace of his character and his Puritan devotion — answered these writings. The Independents generally were not Antinomian, but they accused Dr. Williams of Arminianism, and a fierce quarrel arose between the denominations. Various attempts were made at reconciliation, which only ended in greater bitterness. The controversy raged for some years; Dr. Williams, whose conduct in the dispute was vindicated as wise and fair even by his opponents, closed it with a treatise entitled "Peace with Truth, or an End to Discord." He believed that he had laid down in this book a declaration of principles which would be a sufficient foundation for cordial union, and expected that before long endeavours for denominational unity would be resumed.

Before attempts at a Happy Agreement could be begun again with any hope of success, Unitarianism had become a "burning question" in England. In Exeter, where there were four Presbyterian churches, James Peirce, one of the ministers, adopted anti-Trinitarian doctrine. He did not think it necessary to preach it, but he left out of his services all references to the three persons of the Godhead. A brother minister finding, in conversation with him, what Peirce's sentiments were, proclaimed his lapse from orthodoxy in Exeter, and the news quickly spread among the people. They requested the London ministers—Presbyterian and Independent—to advise them; and the London ministers met to consider the matter in Salters' Hall. A letter to Exeter was determined on; but before it was drafted Thomas Bradbury, an able and vehement Independent, one of the most representative Congregationalists, proposed that every minister then present should, as a witness to his own faith, subscribe the first Article of the Established Church on the doctrine of the Trinity, and the answers to the fifth and sixth questions in the Catechism of the Westminster Assembly. This motion was opposed mainly on the ground that it was an imposition of a human creed, and that to enforce such a creed was inconsistent with the principles of Protestant Dissent. It was rejected by seventy-three to sixty-nine votes, on which the minority, mainly Congregationalists, left the conference and formed themselves into a separate Assembly. The non-subscribing Assembly had some Congregationalist and Baptist members, but its majority was Presbyterian.

The immediate result of all this was, on the

Presbyterian side, an added impulse to Unitarianism; it made the Congregational churches look to detailed doctrinal creeds for that defence of truth which the more consistent Congregationalists now believe the spiritual fellowship sufficient to secure. Nearly all the evangelical Presbyterians gradually became Independents; they had always been Congregational in practice, now they assumed the Congregational name. The possession of property, chapels, manses, endowments, was determined in this way—where the orthodox members seceded, the Unitarians held the trusts; where the Unitarians seceded, the Congregationalists held them. By-and-by litigation arose, and an Act of Parliament was passed ordering that, where no specific doctrines had been laid down in the trust-deed, the property was secured to those who had held it for a term of not less than twenty-five years. The latest decision of the courts, in 1897, is of historical as well as legal interest. The Defoe Memorial Church, in Tooting, received its name because Daniel Defoe had been at one time associated with the congregation. The original deed settling property on the congregation declared it to be for the use of

"Protestant Dissenters of the Presbyterian or Independent denomination." For more than a hundred years the church had been Congregational, with a succession of Congregational ministers. For the greater part of that time the only Presbyterian church claiming to be English was Unitarian, and the Tooting congregation was never other than Evangelical. In 1876 "the Presbyterian Church of England" was formed, mainly consisting of congregations associated with the United Presbyterian and the Free Churches of Scotland. With this newly-formed church the pastor of the Defoe Memorial Church and a portion of the members determined to unite themselves, "believing," as they said in a resolution passed on the 10th December 1879, "that the doctrine and polity of the Presbyterian Church of England are in harmony with the word of God, and knowing that the real and personal property connected with the church at Tooting are of Presbyterian origin." The London Congregational Union contested their right to do this and continue to hold the property, and the case was decided against the pastor and his Presbyterian adherents. The pleadings prepared on both sides were very elaborate; but the ground of the decision was severely simple. The trust-deed provided that the premises were for the use of Protestant Dissenters of the Presbyterian or Independent denomination to worship in; but the "Book of Order and Discipline of the Presbyterian Church of England" made that impossible. "The rules in that book," Mr. Justice Kekewich said, "conflict at every turn with what I understand to be the essential character of the Independent denomination, namely, that each particular church stands alone, independent of every other church, in harmony with them, perhaps, but still independent, self-contained, self-governed. The Book of Order is directly contrary to that position." If the modern Presbyterianism had allowed the freedom which the English Presbyterians enjoyed, the question would have had to be fought out more specifically, and it is by no means certain that the Congregationalists would have won their case. But the rigour of the Scottish method was decisive. The minister was not dismissed, but he was strictly charged that he was not at liberty to continue in his place as a member of the South London Presbytery.

We have two Presbyterian churches in England to-day—this modern "Presbyterian Church of England," which is orthodox, and the old "English Presbyterian Church," which is Unitarian. Its ministers do not use, by choice, the title Unitarian churches; they prefer to call themselves Free or Non-subscribing churches; but many of them cling to the old historic title. Here is the reason that while in America the Unitarians regard with affection the historic name Congregational, their English brethren love the name Presbyterian. The Puritan tradition is very dear to them : they look with reverence to Richard Baxter and Daniel Williams, orthodox though these were; they regard the non-subscribing members of the Salters' Hall conference as their ecclesiastical ancestors.

I have been putting off, all through this Lecture, the consideration of the relation between the Independents of the seventeenth and the Separatists of the sixteenth century. With a word or two on this point I close.

The Independents were not enamoured of the name Separatist or Brownist, and that not simply because it was an offensive title, carrying a stigma with it. They were not true Separatists; had they been so, they would not have sat in the Westminster Assembly, nor entered into Cromwell's purpose of founding a comprehensive National Church. But Baillie and Baxter, and the Presbyterians generally, were not wrong in calling them so. All they knew of Congregational Independency, gathered Churches, discipline, the association of the members with the ministers in church government, the desire for toleration, had been formulated for them by Browne, and Barrowe, and John Robinson, and Henry Jacob, and Henry Ainsworth. The Separatist doctrine was as the leaven, the Independents were the three measures of meal, which in its turn became leaven, leavening the whole lump of English church life. I never study this history, never mark how the habit of gathering for worship outside the Established Churches, and the exercise of care over one another by the members in these separate assemblies, grew into the practice of discipline, and then into an assertion of the doctrine of purity of communion; how the people took into their hands the exercise of government, and found that they were following St. Paul's model in the congregations of the Greek municipalities in Asia Minor and Achaia; how the habit of depending on the guidance of the Holy Spirit led to an assertion of the operative headship of Christ in the churches, which made the thought of civil or ecclesiastical dominion over them intolerable—without recalling some striking words of Mr. Gladstone, when he speaks of the relation of the evangelical revival in the eighteenth century to the Tractarian movement of the ninteenth. "Logical continuity and moral causation are stronger than the conscious thought of man; they mock it, and play with it, and constrain it, even without its knowledge, to suit their purpose."

LECTURE IV

REACTIONS AND REVIVAL

The Act of Toleration—Its Defects—Its Adaptation to the Times—Nonconforming Preachers in Parish Churches—The Power of the Patron—Private Chapels and Chaplains—Charles II.'s Indulgence—Dissenters Excluded from Public Life—Colleges and Grammar Schools Closed to Dissenters—Dissenting Academies—The Corporation and the Test Acts—Occasional Conformity—Profanation of Holy Communion—Nonconformists and the Shrievalty of London—Lord Mansfield on Religious Persecution—Development of Separatism under this Policy—Baxter on the "Lazy" Separatists—Wesley's Censure of Independent Ministers—Dissenting Churches in the Eighteenth Century—Isaac Watts—Philip Doddridge—The Disabling Influence of Smallness—Watts's Patriotism—"A Garden Walled Around"—Indifference to the Spiritual Needs of England a Characteristic of the Eighteenth Century—Decay of Interest in Religion—The Evangelical Revival—Methodism and Puritanism—Calvinistic and Arminian Methodists—Their Church Doctrine—Drift toward Congregationalism—Influence of Methodism on English Religion.

LECTURE IV

REACTIONS AND REVIVAL

THE Act of Toleration was the only solution of the religious difficulty in England which the times and the tempers of men permitted. It was not an ideal Act; it was founded upon that principle of compromise, so dear to the average Englishman and so offensive to the dogmatist. It was niggardly in its concessions, and created new difficulties. It divided the religious part of the nation into two classes— the privileged and the tolerated—and this division became a line of cleavage which has penetrated through every stratum of the social life. It hindered for more than a century the establishment of a national system of education ; the conflict between two sections of educationists —those who want a national and those who want a denominational system—is one of the "burning questions" of to-day. And yet our children, who will read the history more dis-

passionately than we can, may affirm it to have
been, in its result, both beneficent and wise.
It gave a temporary peace if it did not secure
a lasting concord. Certainly it was better than
any Act of Comprehension would have been.
No Act of Comprehension could have effaced
dissent. The thoroughgoing Independents, and
the Baptists, would still have been outside
the National Church. But we should have had
a small dissent, unfit for grappling with problems
as they arose, and powerless to influence statesmen. The Toleration Act made the Dissenters
a large and strong body; much of the learning,
the piety, the social influence of the land was
with them. If the Episcopalians were secured
in their supremacy, the Nonconformists had the
liberty to preach, and to order their churches
according to what they believed to be " the
mind of Christ." This was all that Browne,
and Barrowe, and John Robinson—the early
Separatists—asked for. It was what Milton
regarded as the highest earthly boon. " Give
me the liberty to know, to utter, and to argue
freely according to conscience, above all liberties." I am not at all sure that a much larger
measure of liberty would have been a boon even

to the Independents.   Freedom for thought
cannot be won by a *coup de main*, nor conferred by an Act of Parliament.   It has subtler
enemies than legislation can put down—prejudice, narrowness, want of consideration for
others—and the discipline of the yoke is a
surer solvent of these than social advantages
and easy times.

I

The toleration of Dissenters was according to
the mind of the nation.   The Act of Uniformity
itself had not been able to silence Presbyterian
and Independent ministers, and suppress Congregational church discipline.   Dr. Halley has
told us how " several nonconforming ministers
in Lancashire contrived in one way or another
to retain their places without complying with
the requirements of the Act.   This could be
done only where the minister was so much
respected that no one would lay an information
against him, where the patron of the living had
no desire to present another incumbent, and
generally where the stipend was so small as to
excite no desire in any other clergyman to

I

appeal to authority to have the church declared vacant." [1]

He enumerates thirteen chapelries in Lancashire where the incumbency was not disturbed by the refusal of the clergyman to conform, and says that similar instances of nonconforming ministers retaining their benefices or being allowed to preach in their churches as lecturers, may be found in the adjoining counties of York and Chester.   A chapel at Morley in Yorkshire continues to be occupied by Congregationalists, and a Unitarian congregation still holds " the ancient chapel of Toxteth Park," a suburb of Liverpool.

A state of things like this requires a word or two of explanation. It is partly accounted for by the national character. The well-regulated English mind finds a charm in inconsistency, equal to that which order brings to more servile spirits. We do not cut off the ravelled edges of our fabrics, we twist them into fringes, and account them picturesque. The Englishman is not a rationally

---

[1] " Lancashire ; its Puritanism and Nonconformity," by Robert Halley, D.D.   London: Hodder & Stoughton, 1869. Vol. ii. p. 146.

tolerant man, but he is easy-going. He is
liable to fierce bursts of popular passion, and
the passion while it lasts is ruthless; but it
soon subsides. He

> "Carries anger as the flint bears fire :
>   Who, much enforced, shews a hasty spark,
>   And straight is cold again."

The power of the patron of the living, a
remnant of feudalism, accounts for more. The
lord of the manor had perhaps built the chapel ;
he was responsible for much of the cost of
maintaining the building, the parish clergyman,
and the public worship. He had presented the
incumbent; it would have lain with him to
appoint a successor. There are instances
where, through the favour of the patron,
under Elizabeth's or Charles's Act of Uniformity, a Congregational Church was formed
within the parish, ministered to sometimes by
the parish clergyman, sometimes by a lecturer
acting with his concurrence. Other members
of the aristocracy had private chapels and
private chaplains ; they claimed the right,
both of disregarding the Act of Uniformity in
their own households, and of inviting as many

neighbours as they pleased to their family worship. All the people of a parish might thus have been Congregationalists within the Established Church. Greenwood, the martyr, had been Puritan chaplain to Lord Rich in Essex, and had been allowed by the parish clergyman to minister to a gathered Church at Rochford Hall, until his conscience drove him to London, where he avowed himself a Separatist. In the times of the Evangelical Revival, the Calvinistic section had some aristocratic leaders who unintentionally fostered dissent in this way. The Countess of Huntingdon built chapels, and appointed her chaplains to be ministers of them without the consent of the parish clergyman, and she was very indignant when a legal judgment was given that she could only do so under the Toleration Act, and must register the buildings as dissenting chapels.

We have to consider, also, the tolerant temper of some of the bishops. Bishop Wilkins of Chester, the diocese of which Dr. Halley is writing, definitely allowed this independent action of ministers in a few cases. One reason why the English people prefer Episcopacy to Presbyterianism is, that they believe a bishop acting on his own responsibility more likely to be liberal than a Synod or a Presbytery.

The Court party, moreover, was not consistent in the policy of persecution. Charles II., desiring to propitiate both Romanists and Nonconformists, put out, without consulting Parliament, a Declaration of Indulgence, which practically repealed the Act of Uniformity. A similar Act, in 1687, cost James II. his crown; and there were many Dissenters who, resenting Charles's invasion of the prerogative of Parliament, refused to be indulged. His later declaration, which was issued under Parliamentary sanction, was generally accepted; and it continued in operation until the Toleration Act was passed.

The strength of the Toleration Act was, that it gave legal recognition to a custom which it had been found impossible to repress; its great defect was, that under its operation the Dissenters found themselves excluded from public life. The exemption of Dissenters from " the penalties of certain laws" did not repeal the laws themselves. There were Tory states-

men who avowed that the Toleration Act was
only temporary, and the fear that it might be
so is evidenced by a clause which, during the
whole of the eighteenth century, continued to
be inserted in the trust-deeds of Nonconformist
meeting-houses, directing to what uses the property should be applied should the Toleration
Act be repealed.

The disability imposed by the Act of Uniformity began with the children.   England had
in her colleges and grammar-schools a generous,
and for the time a sufficient, provision for the
scholarly education of her people.   In these
had been trained the great majority of the
clergy, of doctors also and lawyers, as well as
the sons of the gentry, and many farmers'
and tradesmen's sons.   The Act of Uniformity
demanded subscription to the Articles and
Liturgy of the Church from all Heads and
Fellows and Tutors of Colleges, from University Professors and Readers, and masters of
public schools.   There were no old-world conditions to mitigate the pressure of this law.
The schools had not patrons who could have
seen to it that the children of Nonconformists

were not trained up in the practice of the
Established Church ; there was no one in the
universities to protest against the requirement
of subscription to the Thirty-nine Articles when
students entered college and went on to their
degrees.   Under the Toleration Act the Dissenters founded academies of their own, which at
first gave a liberal education to all lads seeking
it, and by-and-by became seminaries for the
training of their ministers.   But these were not
like the old places of learning.   The culture
was generous, and it made scholars, but the
atmosphere was sectarian.   It was as Protestant
Dissenters the young men were taught, and for
the service of their own churches, not as
Englishmen, fired with an ambition to take part
in public life.

The Corporation Act, passed in 1661, imposed
conformity on all town councillors, mayors,
aldermen, and sheriffs, and so excluded Dissenters from municipal office.   Municipal office is
the training-school of public-spirited men : if
it had been intended to dwarf the aspirations
and limit the outlook of a whole section of
English manhood, to make them narrow sectarians, to confine public service to other

sectarians in whom the sense of privilege
should work an equal narrowness of vision,
no surer method could have been devised.
The Test Act, passed in 1673, made the same
demand of conformity on all persons holding
office and emolument from the Crown, on
Ministers of State, on custom-house servants
and excisemen, great and small alike. This
Act, too, kept the sense of injustice constant
in the minds of some of the most devoted
friends of the Commonwealth, and injured the
community by the loss of their service.

The Act of Uniformity, the Corporation Act,
and the Test Act continued in force when the
Act of Toleration was passed, and gave occasion
to some of the bitterest political conflicts of the
eighteenth century. The Whigs were sincerely
attached to toleration, and would have silently
sanctioned any evasion of the restrictive laws to
which Nonconformists might resort; but the
Tories were always for making them stricter,
and for stamping out dissent entirely. John
Robinson had written in favour of the occasional
joining of Separatists in the worship of the
parish churches, although he frankly confessed
that he himself could not practise it. Occasional

conformity was gradually becoming a habit among Dissenters of wealth and social position, of Presbyterian nurture mostly, and it provoked the hostility of the Church and State party, who brought Bills before Parliament to make it illegal. Strong Dissenters, like Defoe and Thomas Bradbury, and the Independents generally, were equally vehement in their opposition to the practice, because it was inconsistent with the integrity of conscience and threatened the absorption of Dissenters into the Established Church. The discussions of the leaders were punctuated by furious riots of the mob, who loved agitation better than they understood the points at issue, and greeted with similar acclamations Sacheverell on his return from condemnation by the House of Lords, and Defoe when he was standing in the pillory. An Act intended to put an end to occasional conformity was passed in 1711; the Schism Bill, preventing any but members of the Established Church from being teachers, became law in 1714. It seemed as if the persecutions of Elizabeth and Charles II. were to be renewed, all the old bitterness was reawakening; Thomas Bradbury wondered—so he said to Bishop

Burnet, when walking through Smithfield—if he should have the constancy and resolution of the old martyrs; and then the death of Queen Anne startled the nation. The whole political prospect was changed; England was delivered from the fear of a Stuart dynasty and a persecuting Church.

The Test and Corporation Acts were not rendered innoxious because there was now no danger of their extension. Thoughtful persons were shocked by the impiety which they encouraged. The profession of the State religion was made by taking the Sacrament within three months of appointment to office, and as part of the qualification. How this degraded the conception of the Lord's Supper, to what scenes it gave occasion, when crowds of successful candidates hung about the churches to qualify, and then went to the ale-house to drink themselves in, may well be imagined. "His Royal Highness Prince Frederick"—so might say a paragraph in the *London Gazette*—"yesterday received the Sacrament, having been appointed Ranger of Windsor Park." There were advertisements of days when the Sacrament would be administered to persons recently admitted to public posts. To this custom Cowper alludes in his satire on the ungodliness and hypocrisy of England.

> " Hast thou by statute shoved from its design
> The Saviour's feast, his own blest bread and wine,
> And made the symbols of redeeming grace
> An office-key, a picklock to a place,
> That infidels may prove their title good
> By an oath dipped in sacramental blood?
> A blot that will be still a blot, in spite
> Of all that grave apologists may write;
> And though a bishop toil to cleanse the stain,
> He wipes and scours the silver cup in vain."

In one historical instance the perversion of the Corporation Act to miserable party purpose at length provoked an appeal to the courts of law. The London City Council being in want of money—they were building the Mansion House, the official residence of the Lord Mayor —for many years chose Nonconformist citizens to be sheriffs. A person refusing to act as sheriff is liable to a fine. In 1742 a citizen declined to qualify for the office by taking the Sacrament, and was cited by the Corporation before the Court of Queen's Bench. The Court decided in the citizen's favour, whereupon the Corporation in 1748 passed a by-law imposing a

penalty of four hundred pounds on any person
who should not accept the Lord Mayor's nomi-
nation, and of six hundred pounds if, after
election by the citizens, he should refuse to
serve. In six years the fines had swelled up to
fifteen thousand pounds, and then resistance
was determined upon. Three Dissenters were in
one year successively elected, and as they would
not pay the fines, the Corporation proceeded
against them in the Sheriff's Court. Judgment
was given in favour of the Corporation, and the
defendants appealed to another local Court,
presided over by the Recorder of London, who
dismissed the appeal. The case was carried
before a special commission of five judges, who,
by a majority of four to one, reversed the
decisions of the Courts below. The Corporation
finally appealed to the House of Lords, and six
judges out of seven gave judgment in favour of
the sole remaining defendant. Lord Mansfield,
the Chancellor, was scathing in his censure of
the Corporation, whom he declared to be not so
much desirous of the Dissenters' services as of
their fines. His summing up contained a defence of liberty of conscience. "There is no
usage or custom," he said, "independent of

positive law, which makes nonconformity a crime. . . . There never was a single instance, from the Saxon times down to our own, in which a man was ever punished for erroneous opinions concerning rites or modes of worship, but upon some positive law. The common law of England, which is only common reason or usage, knows of no prosecution for mere opinions. . . . There is nothing certainly more unreasonable, more iniquitous, more inconsistent with the rights of human nature, more contrary to the spirit and precepts of the Christian religion, more iniquitous and unjust, more impolitic, than persecution. It is against natural religion, revealed religion, and sound policy." The judgment gave heart to the Dissenters; it aroused them to make still further efforts to resist encroachments on their freedom which were not sanctioned by express statute.

Lord Mansfield's distinction between common law and positive law is valuable, but statutes of the realm help to form public opinion. Fighting men, like the Dissenting deputies of London, who organised the resistance to the Corporation, may be alert to see that only such disabilities as are definitely enacted are

enforced upon them. So long, however, as
the Test and Corporation Acts were unre-
pealed, the members of the Church of England
were encouraged in the belief that Dissenters
had fewer natural rights than other people;
and many of themselves, quiet, timid men,
acquiesced in the presumption.

II

The conditions I have been describing, operative for a hundred and fifty years, developed
the Separatist habit in English Nonconformity,
and made the Dissenter the man he was, in
his good qualities and in his defects, at the
beginning of the nineteenth century. Both
the Puritan and the Separatist were strenuous
men. But the strenuousness was of two different types. The Puritan was enthusiastic, ex-
pansive, thinking first of England and the
National Church; the Separatist was intense,
individualistic, aiming at the purity of the
particular Churches in their actual membership. The difference is like that between
spade culture and the use of the plough. The
one produces a heavier and a richer crop per

square yard, but it demands small fields, narrowly hedged in. The other loves large reaches of land, lying open to sun and air, but the crops are not so varied, the individual fruits not so full, nor so finely sent to market. The decay of Presbyterianism meant the gradual death of the larger ambitions; the Churches, instead of the Church, became the supreme object of the care of all Dissenters. Separatism was not regarded with affection by more than a small minority of the English people until the eighteenth century; thoughtful men in the Church of England must sometimes reflect, a little sorrowfully, that but for the Act of Uniformity the Separatists might have died out like the Nonjurors. But the hand of God was in the history; the English ecclesiastical problem could not be solved until this idea of the Church had had full opportunity to prove itself and its worth, to shew what it could do, and wherein, if standing alone, it was doomed to fail.

Richard Baxter, an unsparing critic of the Independents, frequently comments on what seemed to him the exclusive care of their own

members and comparative indifference to the
ungodly who were around them. Here is a
severe sentence from "The Saints' Everlast-
ing Rest"; it is an admonition addressed
to the parish clergy : "Have a watchful eye
upon each particular sheep in your flock; do
not as the lazy Separatists, that gather a few
of the best together, and take them only for
their charge, leaving the rest to sink or swim,
and giving them over to the Divel and their
lusts, and except it be by a Sermon in the
pulpit, scarce ever endeavouring their salvation, nor once looking what becomes of them.
O, let it not be so with you." The same
criticism is still occasionally passed on Nonconformist ministers by pious clergymen of
the Established Church. They look upon
all the residents in the parish as equally
within their cure, and treat them as all alike
members of the Church. It is a heavy responsibility they are bearing; the consciousness of it makes them disposed to judge, as
indifferent to the burden of souls, the ministers
whose sole charge is the fellowship of men and
women like-minded with themselves. John
Wesley uses Baxter's word. In his Diary,

when he records, as he frequently has to do, that some of his preachers become Independent ministers, he taxes them with laziness. Wesley's "parish" was "the world;" he has the zeal for itinerant—Apostolic—preaching which Baxter has for parish visitation; he cannot understand the intensive culture of souls, nor think of men who are not ready to share his special labour as actuated by any other motive than love of ease.

Baxter was comparatively a young man, and a minister of small experience, when he wrote the words I have quoted. Six years after, in "The Reformed Pastor," he speaks differently. Appealing again to the parish clergy, he says: "We do keep up Separation, by permitting the worst to be uncensured in our churches; so that many honest Christians think they are necessitated to withdraw. I must profess that I have spoke with some members of the Separated (or gathered) churches, that were moderate men, and have argued with them against their way, and they have assured me that they were of the Presbyterian judgment, or had nothing to say against it, but they joyned themselves with other churches upon mere

K

necessity, thinking that Discipline, being an ordinance of Christ, must be used by all that can, and therefore they durst no longer live without it when they may have it; and they could find no Presbyterian churches that executed Discipline, as they wrote for it; and they told me that they did thus separate only *pro tempore*, till the Presbyterians will use Discipline, and then they would willingly return to them again. I confess I was sorry that such persons had any such occasion to withdraw, and the least ground for such a reason of their doings. It is not keeping them from the Sacrament that will excuse us from the further exercise of Discipline, while they are members of our churches." In his later years, when he wrote his Autobiography —one of the most interesting of our English classics—he goes still further. He describes his graduated care of his parishioners. His first charge is the members, that is, the recognised communicants; then he thinks of the members of the congregation who are not communicants; afterward, as time and strength will allow, he labours among the parishioners generally who do not come to church. "For the Independents," he says, " I saw that most of them were zealous, and very many learned, discreet, and godly men, and fit to be very serviceable in the church. And I found in the search of Scripture and Antiquity, that in the beginning a *Governed Church*, and a *Stated Worshipping Church*, were all one, and not two severall things . . . and that they were societies of Christians united for *Personal Communion;* and not only for Communion by Meetings of Officers and Delegates in Synods, as many churches in Association be. And I saw if once we go beyond the bounds of *Personal Communion*, as the end of Particular Churches, in the Definition, we may make a Church of a nation, or of ten nations, or what we please, which shall have none of the natural ends of the Primitive particular Churches. Also I saw a commendable care of *Serious Holiness* and *Discipline* in most of the Independent churches."

III

Turning to the biographies of the eighteenth century, we have many charming pictures of dissenting churches. We see small communi-

ties under the affectionate and unwearied care
of godly ministers, living lives of great eleva-
tion, often of singular domestic graciousness
and gravity. The most favoured ministers are
of very moderate means, and the majority are
poor, as are many of the members. But there
is no misery in their poverty; always they
have the Good Shepherd's guidance, in green
pastures, to still waters, and gifts from generous
hands are not wanting. The churches are
rigorously self-sustaining, and watchful over
their poorer members. The students for the
ministry gather together as the family of their
tutor, conducted through a fairly wide range
of human and divine learning, leading in turn
the devotions of the household, encouraged to
preach to the church of which their tutor is
the pastor, and sent out by him to conduct
cottage services. Isaac Watts belongs to them
—the gifted and beautiful boy, a scholar from
his childhood, and never relaxing in his love
of knowledge, soothing the sorrows of a sickly
life with "divine and moral songs," affectionately tending a small church in the city of
London, and living for several years at Stoke
Newington in the country house of Mr. and

Mrs. Elizabeth Abney (afterwards Sir Thomas and Lady Abney), whose beautiful grounds are now the cemetery of Abney Park, the necropolis of London Evangelical Dissenters. Philip Doddridge was another, the country pastor at Kibworth in Leicestershire, then town minister in Northampton, preaching a gracious doctrine that broadened away from Calvinistic orthodoxy, always having students in his home over whom he sedulously watched, writing a family exposition of the Scriptures, and a treatise on the "Rise and Progress of Religion in the Soul," which all Christians loved to read. He, too, was a poet and a valetudinarian. His death at Lisbon, where he was in search of health, the more impressed his memory on his people's hearts. Northamptonshire and Leicestershire still cherish his name with singular reverence, and visitors are shewn relics of him which are religiously preserved. There were less known homes, where ministers lived an obscure but sufficient life—some teachers of boys, others farmers, able to load a haycart with the best; others students of science— natural philosophy, as it was then called— all known for men of God, whom the country round acknowledged at their death to have been worthy of their people's attachment.

But the disabling influence of smallness was upon it all. They were not conscious of it when they were among their books; there they were free of the best society. But they never stepped beyond their own door without being reminded that they were an excluded class. In a different fashion, they felt the contrast between Puritan loftiness of aspiration and Puritan narrowness of opportunity, which made Hawthorne the man he was. As they had not the fret of genius, they did not grow vocal; they simply gave themselves to make the best for God they could of their sunless lives. Their church was the only sphere to which they could give their practical energies when the daily work for daily bread was ended; and they watched its purity, its doctrinal soundness, its zeal for truth, and its devotional temper with a jealousy that was not always wise. The members scrutinised each other's conduct, harassed their children with premature anxieties, became formal in speech and habit. Their younger men grew doctrinaire and controversial, catching at every phantom of free thought, imbibing the social and political doctrines which were preparing for the French Revolution. So, at least, Samuel Wesley says in an evidently prejudiced account of his residence at Mr. Morton's academy in Stoke Newington. The students read books they ought not to have read, lampooned the parish clergyman, and boldly proclaimed king-killing doctrines.

These are dangers inherent in Separatism. In a narrow sphere Independency is not always lovely. Church discipline tends to become vexatious, pragmatic; the meddling man is able to make too much of himself, enlarge the range of practical thought and effort, and Congregationalism is a generous church system, as broad as it is lofty. So John Robinson felt when he counselled the pilgrims to be exiles no longer in a foreign land, but go out and reclaim a country and found a commonwealth of their own. So Henry Jacob felt when he brought back to London some poor fragments of the Amsterdam Church, preferring danger in the nation of which he was a citizen to safety in the land of others. The misery of the Act of Toleration was that under it, for a century, so many Englishmen had ceased to be citizens of England.

In these circumstances Dr. Watts wrote for public worship his Psalms, Hymns, and Spiritual Songs. They are out of date now, and perhaps the book as a whole may never be republished. But they are worth reading, and to the Congregationalist, Congregational habit will continually appear in them. In translating the Psalms, Dr. Watts could not but be patriotic. His patriotism expends itself mostly on two themes — ideal England and spiritual churches. He was not at all a narrow Dissenter, but he had Congregational fellowships in view when he wrote—

> " These temples of his grace,
>   How beautiful they stand !
> The honours of our native place,
>   And bulwarks of our land."

> " Let strangers walk around
>   The city where we dwell,
> Compass and view thine holy ground,
>   And mark the building well :

> The orders of thy house,
>   The worship of thy court,
> The cheerful songs, the solemn vows,
>   And make a fair report.

> How decent and how wise !
>   How glorious to behold !
> Beyond the pomp that charms the eyes,
>   And rites adorned with gold."

There is one of his hymns which Congregationalists used to be charged with always singing; our own speakers are sure to make a point on a platform if they will say, " We no longer love to sing—

" ' We are a garden wall'd around.' "

I have frequently asked Congregational gatherings if any one present ever heard the hymn sung; and no matter how old some of the persons may be, I have not yet seen the man old enough to remember it.   But I do not envy the member of a church who could read only to repudiate such verses as these—

> " We are a garden wall'd around,
>   Chosen and made peculiar ground ;
>   A little spot enclosed by grace
>   Out of the world's wide wilderness.
>
> Like trees of myrrh and spice we stand
>   Planted by God the Father's hand ;
>   And all his springs in Zion flow
>   To make the young plantations grow.
>
> Awake, O heavenly wind, and come,
>   Blow on this garden of perfume :
>   Spirit Divine ! descend and breathe
>   A gracious gale on plants beneath.
>
> Make our best spices flow abroad,
>   To entertain our Saviour God ;
>   And faith, and love, and joy appear,
>   And every grace be active here."

Whatever may be the dignity or the meanness of the stanzas, it should be remembered that English Dissenters had not chosen the condition for themselves. Not from them had come the exclusion, and the narrowness, and the retirement; but it was theirs to look upward for a Heavenly Guest, and to pray that they might be found ready for His visitation.

III

It is not surprising that, under such conditions, the religious needs of the people of England should come to be overlooked, alike when Conformists and Nonconformists were struggling for the mastery, and when both acquiesced in a settlement of their difficulties by compromise. The excitements of the sixteenth and seventeenth centuries gave way to a great lethargy which, in the eighteenth century, affected all the higher life of the nation. Philosophy had become critical instead of constructive; and inevitably a period of scepticism followed, when theology lost its lofty speculative bias, and was wholly devoted to apologetic. Physical science was attracting the more ardent minds, and historical study was reborn ; but metaphysic was discountenanced as leading to no sure result ; the metaphysic of the time was not even educative. Literature had lost imagination ; the *belles lettres* had taken the place of poetry ; the writings of the time are admirable for the clear simplicity of their style ; even the ponderousness of the pulpit died out in the prevailing taste for common sense and lucid utterance. Religious excitement was no longer characteristic of leading men ; Dr. Sacheverell was perhaps a true, he was certainly a squalid, successor to Whitgift and Laud. The mob broke out into frightful excesses, such as that in which Dr. Priestley's library was burnt, and dissenting chapels were wrecked. Notwithstanding these occasional extravagances, the age was not intolerant ; but the tolerance was rather that of exhaustion than largeness in mind and heart. Religion seemed to have decayed with bigotry. Good men were gravely concerned with the apparently universal indifference to serious religion. It is a cheering sign of the times—one that heralded better days—that Churchmen and Dissenters did not accuse each other of being the cause of this spiritual indifference. Doddridge wrote of the decay of the dissenting interest, but it was of spiritual religion, not of denominational influence, he was thinking. Bishop Butler wrote of unbelief as a lamentable feature of the age, not as a consequence of sectarian animosity.

Then came Methodism and the Evangelical Revival, which changed the face of England, and influenced the whole English-speaking world, affecting the destiny of America and the future colonies of Great Britain as markedly as it affected the homeland. Two things are noteworthy about this revival. The movement was not primarily Evangelistic, although it very soon became so. It sprang out of a profound concern for personal godliness, and shewed itself in a longing for deep, inward, spiritual fellowship, such as the Established Church did not contemplate and provide for. The spirit which led the Congregational martyrs, Barrowe, and Greenwood, and Penry, to demand liberty for "gathered churches,"—"the grasp of the great impulse" which drove the Pilgrim Fathers across the sea—was in these Young Oxford Reformers. The early Methodist societies were incipient Congregational churches; the same

craving for mutual edification, not as a pastoral function simply, but as a privilege and
duty of each individual member, appears in
their " method " and in our " discipline." The
Oxford societies of the sixteenth century, which
Mr. Froude so beautifully describes, were re-
peated by John Wesley and his friends ; and
with a similar result. The earlier societies
were contributory to the growth of Separatism ;
the Methodists, too, became Separatists. It
took some of them a long time to learn whither
they were tending, and how God's hand was
impelling them on. Down to the middle of
this century Wesleyan Methodism repelled
the idea of constituting itself a church. There
were secessions from the Wesleyan Societies,
and each secession became a church ; the old
body clung affectionately to the delusion that
its people were still members of the National
Church, claiming a freedom which the bishops
and Parliament would at length confirm them
in. In 1891 the spell was broken ; the
Wesleyan Methodist Church was recognised
by Conference. In 1881 had been held the
first Œcumenical Conference of the Wesleyan
Methodist Churches—of which there are half-

a-dozen in England alone—and in 1892 they joined with Baptists, Congregationalists, and Presbyterians at the Free Church Congress in Manchester, in a common utterance that a Church of Christ is a permanent society of Christian believers, and no others; and that Church fellowship is no accident of nationality, or heredity, but is the mutual communion of all the members.

The next noteworthy fact about the Evangelical Revival is that it sprang out of the Church of England, not out of eighteenth-century dissent. John Wesley was the descendant, through both his parents, of Presbyterian clergymen ejected from their livings on black Bartholomew Day, 1662. His father and mother had voluntarily and conscientiously, and at some cost of feeling, gone back to the establishment before their marriage. The filiation of the present Wesleyan Methodist Church to the old Puritanism of the Presbyterian type is more than the accident of its founder's parentage. It is Presbyterian in its government, Puritan in ecclesiastical habit. There is no inherent antagonism in it to the theory of a National Church; many Wesleyan

Methodists would probably prefer the machinery of such a Church if it left them freedom of spiritual movement ; and they would not regard the two conditions as incompatible. The patience with which Cartwright and Baxter bore with the imperfections of the National Church, its petty interferences, sometimes its malignant persecution, hoping against hope that there would be found a place for them within its constitution, was like that of Wesley. And the reason was the same, not love of ease, or of consideration, but the deep conviction that a National Church gave a gospel minister such opportunities and advantages for the full exercise of his ministry as no other Church relation could furnish. Baxter and Wesley were very unlike in more than their theology—and I confess that I am much more attracted by the personality of Baxter than by that of Wesley—but I cannot read over Baxter's reasonings on such subjects as the Christian ministry, the spiritual needs of a people, and the methods in which they may best be supplied, without having before me the picture of Wesley in action.

IV

The term "Methodism" in the nineteenth century came to connote two ideas—Arminianism in doctrine, and Connectionalism in government; but in the eighteenth century it was not so. George Whitefield, a pronounced Calvinist, was a Methodist. The Countess of Huntingdon's connection was Methodist, but her ministers were almost all Calvinists. There were within the Established Church many clergymen who were commonly called Methodists; some of them, like Rowland Hill, founded separate congregations without repudiating their Episcopal orders; others, like John Newton, and Scott the commentator, and Romaine the preacher, never extended their ministry beyond the parish churches, but they were styled Methodists, while retaining their benefices. These were for the most part Calvinists. The peculiarity of all Methodists, Calvinist and Arminian alike, was that in a certain vague way they recognised three senses of the word Church—the National visible Church, the Church universal and invisible, and a *tertium quid*, an invisible but partly recognisable body of the faithful within the parish churches. John Wesley organised these true believers, on confession of their desire " to flee from the wrath to come," into societies under the direction of the itinerant preachers, which societies were divided up into classes meeting weekly under the charge of godly men and women, whom the preachers appointed. These societies came to have separate places of meeting built for them. At first the members were careful to meet at other hours than those appointed for public worship in the parish churches; in all ways Wesley took care to impress on them the fact that these were not companies of Dissenters, but members of the Established Church, supplementing the national observance by gatherings for their mutual edification. The Countess of Huntingdon encouraged the formation of such societies, and made them more pastoral. She founded a college for the training of ministers who should watch over and direct them. Some of her students received Episcopal ordination, and carried on their work in the parish churches; others became non-Episcopal ministers and met their followers in chapels which she erected for them. There were many of the Established

clergy in general sympathy with the men of the
Revival, who did not form these societies; they
preached to the parish congregation as if it were
a gathered church, and watched over the parish
in the spirit and manner of Richard Baxter.
This was the origin of the Evangelical party
within the Established Church, a body which
for half a century exercised perhaps the greatest
religious influence on the domestic life of
England.

All these new forces, originating in the
Oxford Revival, told directly on English
Congregationalism, adding to its numbers, en-
riching its experience, broadening its purpose,
enlarging its activities. On the other hand, the
existence of the Congregational churches supplied Methodism with an example of free
religious communities, and a norm of church
doctrine. John Wesley tried his best to hold in
check the inevitable development of his societies
into a dissenting church, but in vain. He was
continually losing preachers who found the
itinerant system burdensome and inefficient,
and who became Congregational pastors, bringing an Arminian leaven into Independency.
He was forced to gather his preachers into a

conference, who undertook the charge of the societies, repeating, with some variation, and with more success, the effort of the Puritans to organise religious communities from the Synod and Presbytery downward; repeating also the Puritan experience that Christ's freemen will not always endure to be a governed body, that a voluntary church must ultimately become self-administrative. Each secession from Wesleyanism—and there have been half-a-dozen—has given more and more representation to the lay members. Some Primitive Methodists frankly confess that they have more in common with Congregationalists than with the old body. There are Independent Methodists, retaining their Arminianism, but Congregational in government. Another of these communities is known as the United Methodist Free Churches—not church—and its representative body has abandoned the old Methodist name—Conference or Connexion—for the Congregational term — Assembly. Nearly every congregation founded by the Countess of Huntingdon has become an Independent church. Finally, the Wesleyan Methodist Conference has ceased to be a merely clerical body. Hampered by legal restrictions, and made to move slowly by the fears of the older men, the Conference has added lay representatives to its sessions, and these are acquiring an equal as well as a real power of control.

In a large number of cases the death of a fervid Evangelical parish clergyman was followed by the formation of a Congregational church; in a few cases the Evangelical clergyman became a Congregational minister. A training school for Evangelists, founded by the Reverend John Eyre, of Homerton, and nominated by Rowland Hill to be the residuary legatee of his estate, is now Hackney College. A similar institution, founded at Trevecca by the Countess of Huntingdon, is now Cheshunt College. The principals, professors, and students of both these colleges are generally, though not by legal compulsion, Congregationalists.

One or two interesting marks of this transition period will strike the literary student. Take up, for instance, a copy of John Wesley's Hymn-Book, as he left it, and read the head-lines. You will find "The Society" and "Believers" where, in other Hymn-Books, you would find "The Church." Take up a copy

of Watts's Hymns, and you will not find the
word "Chapel." He has entitled the hymn
"How pleased and blessed was I," for instance,
"On going to Church." The word chapel was
not, in his time, commonly used by Congregationalists. Its subsequent prevalence marks
the influence of Methodism on English Nonconformity; the chapel was a building, supple-
mentary of and subordinate to the parish
church. The old Congregational word in
England, as in America, was meeting - house,
or meeting; the modern term in England, as
in America, is church.

V

The exclusive spirit has gone from Independency not to return. Many causes have been
at work to produce this change—the growth
of the nation, with the new problems that
growth has brought with it; the broadening
of all human thought; the feeling which has
come with increasing consciousness of the
limitations of certainty that dogmatism is
absurd, inhuman; the enlarging charity of
life; but the first impulse came from Method-

ism and the Evangelical Revival. To a considerable extent English Congregationalism has been modified by the number of Methodist preachers who, from the first and down to the present, have come into our ministry. The example of the Methodists is, moreover, a stimulus to every Christian society in the land. But the spirit of Methodism is mightier than its men. All the churches in England are penetrated by the deep conviction that their obligations are not limited to their own adherents; the church may be "gathered," "particular," "separate," but the sphere of their work, and therefore their responsibility, is national, world-wide. "Go and make disciples of all the nations."

LECTURE V

CONGREGATIONALISTS AND ANGLICANS IN THE NINETEENTH CENTURY

Removal of Nonconformist Disabilities in the Nineteenth Century—Influence of the long Struggle on Nonconformist Character—Emancipation of England—The Franchise—Local Councils—Dissenters Liberals in Politics—Is this to be regretted?—Abatement of Controversial Bitterness—Formation and Motive of the Liberation Society—Prevalence and Decay of Individualism—Congregational Individualism—Effect of this on Theology—The Doctrine of the Church—The Oriel School and Congregationalists—John Henry Newman—"Ideal of a Christian Church"—The Church a Voluntary Society—Defects of this Definition—The Separatist Doctrine of the Church recovered—The Broad Church—Thomas Arnold—Frederick Denison Maurice—His Influence on young Congregationalists—Christ's Headship of the Human Race—Maurice and Dale—Congregationalists and Synods—English Congregationalists' Dislike of Councils—Organisation of the Congregational Churches—The "Small Private Church" and the Nation.

LECTURE V

CONGREGATIONALISTS AND ANGLICANS

I

THE nineteenth century witnessed the removal of nearly all the disabilities under which English Nonconformists laboured, through the Act of Uniformity and those specific Acts which were passed to shut them out of public life. The repeal of the Test and Corporation Acts in 1828 allowed them to accept municipal office and to enter the Civil Service. The University Tests Act, passed in 1871, completed a series of changes by which they could go to college, matriculate in the universities, and take their degrees; the grammar schools have been opened to them as pupils and under-masters, though the head-masterships are still to a considerable extent confined to clergymen of the Established Church. An Act for the Registration of Marriages, in

1836, enabled them to be married in their own places of worship and by their own ministers. An Act for the Registration of Births and Deaths, passed the same year, facilitated the introduction of a subsequent measure by which they can bury their dead in the graveyards of their parishes and in the consecrated part of the public cemeteries, without the service of the Established Church. The slowness of their emancipation, even under favourable circumstances, is illustrated by the fact that this latter Bill did not become law until 1880. The disability removed by the public registration of births was so petty, so significant of the bigotry which watched over every section of life, that it deserves a somewhat fuller notice. Up to 1836 the regular way of proving age was the production of a certificate of baptism. When a policy of Life Assurance was to be paid, when lads entered some public offices, when personal identity was to be established, or a passport for foreign travel was applied for, the baptismal certificate had to be produced; and if it was not forthcoming, some one had to be hunted up who remembered the birth, and his or her—generally her—affidavit was grudgingly accepted instead. So deeply had this custom rooted itself in English habit, that the London University, founded in 1837 as a Liberal university, priding itself on its complete ignoring of the religious beliefs of its members, asked matriculating students for their baptismal certificates. All Dissenters found this constant requirement vexatious; to Baptists, Quakers, Jews, and Sceptics it seemed insulting and profane.

The story of this century of emancipation is, to those who took part in it, a matter of pride. Our children, and freemen not natives of England, will wonder—not altogether admiringly—at the patience which could make men endure such ignominy so long. The Act of Toleration made it possible. The religious Dissenter—and the burden bore most heavily on him—had his chapel, his times of social worship, his fellowship with persons like-minded to himself. Some qualities of English Nonconformists will be better appreciated as we recall the story—their intense love of their Churches, their strenuousness and vigilance, their faith in little communities, and their habit of not despising "the day of small things"; their passion for liberty, the deep indignation against all unnecessary restrictions under which their thought about the rights of conscience broadened, so that they who began by asking toleration for themselves became the advocates of a universal toleration, and secured for the Jew, the Roman Catholic, and the unbeliever the same rights as their own. The conventicle did this great work for England. When the phrase "the consolations of religion" is used on the platform and in the press, it generally refers to a man's comfort in dying. The Nonconformist found "the consolations of religion" effective for life; they gave him patience, forbearance, hope; he used what liberty he had, and in no revolutionary temper, but, unwearied and ever watchful, he sought for more.

In a larger sense, the nineteenth century may be called the century of the emancipation of England. Its greatest achievement was the passing of the first Reform Bill in 1832. Up to that time the franchise, national and municipal, was not regarded as the right of the English people: it had come to be the privilege of the few. Parliament was originally a

Council called together to advise the king. The county franchise represented the ancient right of occupiers of land to be represented in this Council; as towns grew some of them were summoned at the royal pleasure to send their members to the House of Commons. The privilege was not at first highly valued; indeed, there were boroughs which asked to be relieved of the burden, because of the cost and trouble it imposed on them. While the power of Parliament developed, the privilege increased in value. The idea of privilege was intensified by the growth of tradition and the pride of the old historic boroughs. The municipal franchises had grown out of trade guilds, and privileges granted by special charters, which charters were conferred by lords of manors as well as by the Crown. In the breathing time of the eighteenth century men had begun to see that England was a people, and that old feudal customs, which had sprung out of the needs of localities, did not meet the case. The enfranchisement of new boroughs had long ceased: the Crown did not want them; the Stuarts would have been glad to do away with Parliaments altogether. Parliamentary and municipal corporations had not followed the distribution of the population. Large towns, like Manchester and Birmingham, sent no members to Parliament; the owner of a manor, like Old Sarum, or the inhabitants of a couple of farm-houses, like Gatton, did. There were many important and growing towns in which there was no corporation at all; there were some in which the mayor and aldermen were nominated by the lord of the manor, and his court leet was in place of a town council. Within the boroughs and counties the franchise was restricted, and it was not uniform; there were freemen of boroughs; freemen of companies— Goldsmiths, Fishmongers, Cordwainers, Loriners, Spectacle-makers, &c., &c.—in London; and all over the country there were scot-and-lot voters, potwallopers, faggot voters, and others, every name representing an original distinction in the qualification, or a variation introduced into the claim. "Fancy franchises," as they were called, were defended by Mr. Disraeli with characteristic affectation, on the ground that they extended the privilege of voting in a picturesque, traditional manner.

All this complicated structure, venerable and

decaying, has been swept away. Reform Bill
has followed Reform Bill, until we have now
the whole country covered with electoral districts, and the franchise given practically to
every male person of full age who pays rates
and taxes; and Councils—town, county, district, urban, and rural—which have put local
public concerns under the direction of the
people of the locality. The most beneficial
result of this extension of the franchise has
been the change it has wrought in men's conception of what the power of voting means.
The process has been educative; it has called
public spirit into play and developed patriotism. The idea that the franchise is a privilege
gave way to the demand for it as a right,
and this gradually passed into the feeling and
conviction that it is a responsibility, a great
public trust.

II

The emancipation of the Dissenters and the
emancipation of England went on side by side,
each movement helping the other. Hence it
has come about that nearly all Dissenters are
identified with the Liberal party. There is a

natural, a psychological affinity between the two causes. English Conservatives may be defined as defenders of privileges, and English Liberals as asserters of rights. The political agitations of two hundred and fifty years have illustrated the sameness of conviction in Liberals and Dissenters, and welded them into one party. The alliance has its disadvantages. We sometimes wish, for religious reasons, that the churches should be entirely free from political prejudice, but it has worked well for the national life. Whig historians of the eighteenth century put the matter somewhat cynically. Sir John Dalrymple, speaking of the failure of William the Fourth's Comprehension Bill, by which the Presbyterians would have been included in the National Church, tells us: "There were a few in Parliament of firm minds and remoter views, who, reflecting that the dissenting interest had been always as much attached to liberty as the Church of England had been to prerogative, thought that opposition and liberty would be buried in the same grave, and that great factions should be kept alive, both in Church and State, for the sake of the State itself." Speaker Onslow condemns this maxim, not too severely : " A false and foolish notion, the artifice of mean and weak politicians, who value themselves upon small cunning, and think, or hope at least, that it will be deemed wisdom." Mr. Green, whose " History of the English People " is not cynical, speaks of the failure of the Comprehensive Bill as of the highest political value. " The Toleration Act established a group of religious bodies whose religious opposition to the Church forced them to support the measures of progress which the Church opposed. With religious forces on the one side and on the other, England has escaped the great stumbling-block in the way of nations where the cause of religion has become identified with that of political reaction."

These struggles for religious equality have, however, left very little ill-feeling behind them; as reform after reform has been carried, political conflict has become larger minded, and religious controversy more gracious. A body of young Oxford Churchmen threw themselves into the agitation for opening the universities, declaring that the nation suffered more when citizens were shut out from the higher culture than did the excluded parties, and that Uni-

M

versity reform should contemplate the admission of poor men as well as Nonconformists. The latest Bill for freeing Dissenters from annoyances in the use of the parish graveyards was introduced in the House of Commons by a Churchman and Conservative. A few disabilities yet remain, mostly in the operation of the Education Acts. It is probable they will be settled by common agreement, by discussion rather than by controversy. Platform invective and newspaper bitterness are not now the characteristics of English religious difference; where they appear they are found as superstitions, bad habits remaining over from ignorant times.

III

In 1844 the Anti-State Church Association was formed, for the definite purpose of securing self-government to all Churches, and of freeing Parliament, which had now become the Council of the Nation, representing citizens, and not sectaries, from the necessity of legislating in the interests of a single church. The enfranchisement of England had prepared the way for this movement, and it came about when Dissenters

grew conscious of their political strength. But
it was in essence a deeply religious movement.
It was the full logical expression of the Separatist conscience of the sixteenth century, and all
the struggles of the seventeenth and eighteenth
centuries made it inevitable. The Presbyterian
Independents of the eighteenth century did not
deem a State Church necessarily inconsistent
with religious liberty. Even such a man as
Doddridge could say that he had "always
pleaded for the reasonableness of submitting to
a majority here, and of our being obliged,
though we are Dissenters, to do our part towards maintaining that clergy which the
authority of our country in general has thought
fit to establish; and indeed, so far as I can
judge, it is admitted by all but the Quakers,
whose opposition is now mere matter of form."
The controversy over the Occasional Conformity
and Schism Bills had perhaps more to do than
any other single cause with the changed mind
of Dissenters in the nineteenth century. The
attaching of special civil privileges to a special
religious profession was manifestly degrading
the religious profession itself; it obscured the
principle admirably expressed by Robert Browne

—" the Lord's people are of the willing sort."
The ease with which men could flatter themselves into the belief that they were true
Christians because they observed the religious ordinances which Parliament sanctioned
prompted Mr. Binney to say that the Established Church system " destroyed more souls
than it saved." The sense of civil justice was
confused in many good men's minds by their
habitual tendency to defend the political action
of governments that secured them their favoured
religious position. The officials of the Church
of England as a whole were in favour of the
American War ; they opposed the abolition of
slavery, the repeal of the Corn Laws, and the
abandonment of the penalty of hanging for
small offences. The Dissenters were amazed at
the rancour with which clergymen opposed their
admission to the universities, the conferring on
them the right to marriage and burial by their
own ministers, and generally the extension to all
subjects of the full advantages of Englishmen.
They knew that most of these clergy were good,
kind-hearted men ; they respected many of
them for their piety and their devotion to their
calling. When they asked themselves how such

men could sanction selfishness and injustice, they could only assign as the reason that their position in a Church specially associated with a State was radically false. Mr. Edward Miall expressed the most solemn conviction of nine-teenth century Nonconformists when he affirmed again and again that their object was not so much the liberation of Dissenters as the libera-tion of Christianity, of religion. It was to express this idea that the old name " Anti-State Church Association," dear to Radical reformers as a fighting title, was changed in 1853 to the graver and more fully descriptive name, " Society for the Liberation of Religion from State Patron-age and Control." From the first the English Nonconformists had the Scottish Voluntaries with them ; the Free Church of Scotland, which originally testified to the need of a national provision for religion, had accepted the Libera-tion principle before it joined with the United Presbyterians in one Church. Slowly but effectually the doctrine is influencing the more earnest members of the Church of England itself.

IV

The advancing work of emancipation has had
one result, as unpremeditated as it has proved
in its action to be benignant; it has taken away
that confidence in individualism which, in the
early years of the century, characterised our
foremost publicists. The claim of liberty used
to be put in this form : every man has naturally
the right to perfect freedom of action, in so far
as he does not encroach on the rights of others.
The definition did not contemplate any right
in society to secure that the individual should
be trained for the duties of citizenship. The
demand for a system of national education was
resisted, not only by members of the extreme
right, who were afraid that to educate the
children of the poor would make them dis-
contented, but also by members of the extreme
left, who would not have the authority of the
parent over his children interfered with. These
persons honestly believed that the sense of
parental obligation would be weakened if the
State provided public schools and made children
attend. Mr. Bright opposed the Mines and
Factories Acts, which fixed the age at which

children were set to work and the conditions of
their labour, because it was not consistent with
the rights of parents. He spoke against an Act
to prevent adulteration of articles of food, because he dreaded the intrusion of Government
inspectors into a shopkeeper's book-keeping.
Our later legislation has defied such criticism.
Not only are schools now provided at the
public cost, but museums, art galleries, circula-
ting and reference libraries, parks and play-
grounds, baths and wash-houses as well.
Corporations are empowered to purchase and
destroy dwelling-houses in crowded districts,
and to build houses for the poor. Private
monopolies and the monopoly of companies are
checked by the powers of municipalities to
supply tramways and omnibuses, gas and water
and electric power, for the use of the inhabitants. These enlargements of State action were
at first suspiciously watched; but the movement
has been irresistible. Sir William Harcourt's
phrase—"We are all socialists now"—is not
strictly accurate, but it is the vivid declaration
of a fact. To rejoice in this alteration of the
national habit is not necessarily to condemn the
older individualism. That individualism was

not selfish; Bentham and Malthus were as true philanthropists as Carlyle and Ruskin. Its error was that it mistook a temporary necessity for an abiding social condition. The possibility of individual development is as much a right of man as freedom of individual action, and this by common consent the State is setting itself to secure. Socialism itself has been modified by the new environment; the former demand of equal conditions for all men has given way to the claim of equal opportunities. This formula will be seen to be as narrow as was the other; indeed, even now, probably, it does not mean all it says; it is really the claim of room and provision for every person to develop himself according to his powers, and to fit himself, as fully as he can, to render his own service to the community.

No keener, more conscientious individualists have ever been than were the English Congregationalists—Baptist and pædo-Baptist—of the first half of the nineteenth century. Their characteristic Church doctrine was that the sphere of religion was limited to personal thought and action, from which sphere the State was to be rigidly excluded. Hence their objection to a national system of education. Education, they said, is not instruction, but the training of the personality. The doctrine of the old-fashioned Voluntaries was that no way was to be found of distinguishing between education and religion, and that religion included dogma; and that therefore to give education was one of those inward, personal obligations with which the State must not interfere.

Their circumstances had made them the individualists they were. Shut away from public life, deprived of the social advantages provided by pious benefactors of the past, they had not only thriven in temporal affairs; they had developed manliness of spirit and the godly habit. They had won their emancipation by their own patient endeavour. We need not wonder if the consciousness of all this made them oblivious of two other facts, first, that not all persons could do as they had done: and secondly, that such as they were, they were not wholly their own creation; that the solidarity of the nation had been operative even upon them, that their very personality was English, that their obligations were social, as was every advantage they enjoyed. Their religion was individualistic; per-

sonal election to personal salvation was the note
of the Calvinist; the notes of the Evangelical
Revival were personal repentance, conscious
faith, the obedience of the personal will. The
tendency to individualism received a great impulse from "the Voluntary Controversy" in
Scotland. Originally, this discussion turned on
the point of pecuniary support; should churches
be sustained and ministers paid by free-will
offerings or by endowments and public money;
but the word Voluntary gradually insinuated
itself into every department of Church life. A
Christian Church was commonly defined as "a
voluntary association of believers in Christ for
mutual edification and the advancement of the
Kingdom of God." Other aspects of the Christian fellowship had fallen into oblivion—the
organic piety of which Dr. Bushnell made so
much; the membership in the body of Christ
which is prior to the personal profession; the
limitation of the right to multiply small communities by regard to the Catholic oneness;
the fact that Christian social obligations are
only recognised, not constituted, by the act of
the individual. The whole Christian life took
on a tone of hardness from this individualism.

The Evangelical theology was rationalistic ; the lofty mysticism, which is the charm of the seventeenth century Puritan doctrine, was lacking. Its apologetic was ineffective, as apologetic in which there is no mystic element must ever be. The Atonement became a scheme for overcoming governmental difficulties which the fact of sin had introduced ; not the outflowing of the Heavenly Father's heart. The divine righteousness was defined as the giving to every man exactly what he had deserved ; and no ingenuity has been able to evolve a consistent doctrine of sacrifice out of that. The solidarity of man, Christ's Headship of the human race, not figurative or forensic, but real, vital, was not thought of, only His personal forgiveness of the individual penitent, the justification of the individual believer. The *Testimonium Spiritus Sancti* became, first, a doctrine of personal assurance merely, and then was seldom preached at all. Among Congregationalists the word Sacrament fell into disuse ; instead, persons spoke of ordinances ; and the very conception of the two Christian rites was impoverished. No witness to organic unity, in nature and grace, was seen in baptism ; it was regarded, almost wholly, as a confession of personal faith or a dedication of children to God. The Lord's Supper was a commemoration rather than a communion; and the commemoration was the recalling of the fact and meaning of His sacrificial death; the higher, larger truth that it is a witness to His perpetual bestowal of the grace of His glorified humanity on His people was scarcely apprehended.

V

The first impulse to a more generous and Catholic doctrine of the Church among modern Congregationalists came—so I at least believe —from a movement which they regarded with intense suspicion and dislike; the new High Churchism, which was identified with Oriel College, Oxford, and which culminated in the publication of the "Tracts for the Times." Dr. Newman has told us in his *Apologia Pro Vita Sua*, that he was repelled from the Evangelicism in which he had been brought up by his fear of Liberalism; and by Liberalism he means that extreme Individualism which I have been describing. Newman has had no direct, abiding influence on English Nonconformity; it was impossible that any one who calls the light of day "garish," as he does in his hymn, "Lead, kindly light," should persuade men who value "the liberty to know, to utter, and to argue freely according to conscience, above all liberties." They felt the piety of his temperament, and the charm of his lucid English; but they perceived the subtlety of that apparently clear style, and they altogether repudiated his doctrine of economy in the statement of truth. His use of the doctrine of development repelled them, because it was development Romeward; but they saw that, both in the history of the Church and in the promises of Christ, development of Christian truth was an essential part of God's spiritual providence; and they sympathised with his ceaseless demand of freedom for the Church to develop according to its own law, unfettered by State legislation and the fancied necessities of worldly societies. W. G. Ward's "Ideal of a Christian Church" is full of passionate longings for ecclesiastical autonomy; and Congregationalists reawoke to the perception that, in their own churches, the autonomy, the liberty of development, under the guidance of

Christ's Spirit, existed in its highest, purest
form. They saw, too, that the doctrine of development involved the continuity and identity
of the Christian consciousness; involved the
historic Church, not to be confounded with
Rome, or England, or any ecclesiastical establishment, but also not to be dismissed as invisible, ideal merely. Under the influence of
this thought, too, they studied their own system
of government; and they saw that Congregationalism provided for Catholicity, as well as for
autonomy, in its highest, purest form.

Such were the conceptions taking form in
the minds of young men in our colleges in
the middle of the last century; many of the
students of those days have since become denominational leaders, and they have restored
the old lofty Separatist doctrine of the Churches
and the Church. A few of them have lately
called themselves High Church Congregationalists; a title I do not love, but they mean
by it, that they have a doctrine of the Church,
as clear, consistent, gracious and commanding,
as any held by Romanist or Anglican. Memory
may deceive a man in advancing years, and I
would not claim absolute historical accuracy

for all I am now saying. But I have a vivid impression that, while I often heard in youth sermons on the importance of the Christian ministry, I seldom heard a sermon on the Christian Church; and when I did so, it was the meagre presentation of a voluntary society, charged with the obligation of maintaining its own purity of communion, while its members did all the good they could. Listening to a preaching friar in Milan Cathedral, I was won by the passionate fervour with which he spoke of the bark of St. Peter, and dilated on the unity, sanctity, catholicity, and apostolicity of the Church. I thought to myself—" We too, we Congregationalists, have a doctrine of the Church, which we hold dear as God's truth; how is it that we leave Romanists and Anglicans to preach on this theme with fervour? how is it that with all our zeal for purity and apostolicity we do not make our congregations glow as we discourse on unity and catholicity?" That hour in Milan Cathedral has affected my whole ministry; and I found that many of my contemporaries were passing through a similar experience. Apostolicity—we follow the model laid down by the Apostles; sanctity

—we seek it in assemblies of holy men and women; unity—the Christian consciousness is the same and constitutes one spiritual community of believers in every age; catholicity—we value the separate fellowship of believers because we want no organisation between them and the whole family in earth and heaven, and will not substitute for that communion the meaner figure of a big institution.

When the Congregationalist of to-day turns back to the early Separatist writings, he discovers that he has more in common with Browne and Barrowe, and Jacob and Ainsworth, and Robinson, than with the Individualists of the first half of his own century. With the older men as with him, the Church comes first, the individual member second. The difference is not great in the particular truths; it is great in the proportion and relative incidence of the truths. It would be easy to multiply quotations; I will content myself with two or three from Robert Browne. "The Church planted or formed is a company or number of Christians or believers, which, by a willing covenant made with their God, are under the government of God and Christ, and keep his laws in one holy communion." "The Church government is the Lordship of Christ in the communion of his offices; whereby his people obey to his will and have mutual use of their graces and callings, to further their godliness and welfare." This is much better than the nineteenth Article of the Church of England—"The visible church of Christ is a congregation of faithful men, in the which the pure Word of God is preached, and the Sacraments be duly ministered according to Christ's ordinance in all those things that of necessity are requisite to the same"—because it lays stress, not on order, but on the living Lordship of Christ, and on the communion of offices, "whereby his people have mutual use of their graces and callings." It is also better than the prevailing definition among Congregationalists sixty years ago, the "Voluntary association" definition, because it makes the covenant with God the voluntary act; where the will has been yielded to God, the association is of spiritual inevitableness rather than of personal determination. Browne, moreover, speaks of the Church—and he means the particular, not merely the ideal, universal Church—as having

N

"the communion of those graces and offices, which are in Christ;" "it hath the use of his priesthoode, because he is the High Priest thereof. Also of his prophecie, because he is the Prophet thereof; also of his kingdome and government, because he is the Kynge and Lorde thereof." He speaks of Christ as using "the obedience of his people" for the fulfilment of these offices; and goes on to indicate how all Christians are made Kinges and Priestes. We are Kings because "we must all watch each other, and trie out all wickedness;" "Christians are Priestes unto Christ, because they present and offer up praiers unto God, for themselves and for others. They turn others from iniquitie, so that atonement is made in Christ unto justification. In them also and for them others are sanctified, by partaking the graces of Christ unto them." This is very different from the conception of Christian Kingship as self-control, and of priesthood as the right of every man to say his own prayers.

VI

The Tractarian revolt against Protestantism was followed at once by a counter movement— the rise of the Broad Church School, which, during the middle third of the century, powerfully affected English thinking on religious and social subjects. One of its first teachers was Dr. Arnold, who did not materially modify Congregational thought; a little later came the prophet of the movement, Frederick Denison Maurice, who did. Maurice was a child of the eighteenth century Presbyterianism; his father was a typical Unitarian, having so large a regard for liberty of conscience that he did not try to impress his own theological beliefs on his children, combined with an intensity of personal conviction that saddened his later years when his family left him alone in his religion. His three eldest daughters became Calvinists, as did his wife. "In one of her letters to her husband," Frederick Maurice's son and biographer has written, "she announces her conviction that 'Calvinism is true.' The contrast to the form in which her daughters announced their adhesion to the sect which

they joined is very remarkable. For the very
essence of Calvinism in the sense of her letter
is this : That it assumes the existence in the
world of a select body who are known as 'the
elect'; and assumes further that every one in
the world can determine in his own mind
whether or no he possesses a certain *testamur*
which is called 'faith,' by which he can decide
whether or no he belongs to that select body.
Now, on the one hand, each of the sisters quite
willingly gave the accredited proofs of their
possessing the *testamur* in question, and on
the other, Mrs. Maurice never satisfied herself
that she could do so, though looking at the
matter from the outside she quite believed that
this view of the universe was the correct one."
The biographer adds : "It is scarcely too much
to say that such a position is a contradiction in
terms." This comment would not have been
written by any one who had a large acquaintance with English Puritan biography, in which
the want of this personal assurance on the part
of those who were most deeply persuaded of
the truth of the system is a constant and
pathetic feature; or with the rise of anti-
Calvinistic Methodism, which gives personal

assurance a prevalence which it lacked in English Calvinism. But there is little doubt that the biographer had learnt what he wrote on this subject from his father. The difference between the daughters and the mother seems to have been mainly a matter of temperament. " The intense individuality of each of their characters " — I am again quoting from the biography—" the dramatic distinctness of the personality of each of these three sisters, is to be noted also of every separate member of the whole family. It is the one sure mark of the race that seems to have been noticed by all who knew them. It gave to their peculiarities of religious conviction an earnestness and a certain aggressiveness which, despite their general agreement on the main point of Calvinism, showed itself in the discussions with one another, not always in an attractive form." Under these incidents of his home life, the elder Maurice himself revealed the intensity of his character, and questioned whether he had been a wise and faithful father in leaving his children so much as he had done to the religious guidance of others.

Frederick Maurice's boyhood was passed in

this atmosphere of religious controversy, and it determined the sentiment of his life. "The desire for *Unity*," he says, "has haunted me all my life through; I have never been able to substitute any desire for that, or to accept any of the different schemes for satisfying it which men have devised." And his son thus interprets the sentence: "In other words, the great wish in the boy's heart was to reconcile those various earnest faiths which the household presented." To this "desire for Unity" Frederick Maurice attributes his becoming a member of the Church of England. "I not only believe in the Trinity in Unity, but I find in it the centre of my beliefs, the rest of my spirit when I contemplate myself and mankind. But strange as it may seem, I owe the depth of this belief in a great measure to my training in my home. The very name that was used to describe the denial of this doctrine is the one which most expresses to me the end that I have been compelled, even in spite of myself, to seek." This is a very significant utterance; the reconciliation of apparent antinomies was the master motive of his life.

It is just here that we see the secret of the

influence which Maurice came, afterward, to exercise on young Congregationalists. It was not because he had any sympathy with them; he displays a singular want of appreciation of their position. He repudiated their demand for the rights of the individual conscience interpreted by the individual judgment; and he was repelled by even the modified form in which Evangelicals spoke of personal experience. The controversy between him and men like Dr. John Pye Smith and Dr. Wardlaw has a bitterly intolerant spirit, from which Maurice, in his early days, was not free. His "Kingdom of Christ" is painful reading, alike to those who love him and to those who love Congregationalism. It is dogmatic, one-sided in statement, perverse in temper. In later years the harshness became softened, but the intolerance remained. Under the influence of Thomas Erskine, of Linlathen, he learned to understand Calvinism better; but his narrow judgment of the Separatist testimony never left him. Just as the typical Dissenter of that period saw everywhere in the Bible a condemnation of the identification of Church and State, so Maurice saw in it from first to last a condemnation of those who thought that, in Christian fellowship, the godly should separate themselves from the godless. His exegesis is continually turning on this one point; no literalist is more confident in his quotation of Scripture than is this broad-hearted man when he reads his own thought into the stories of Genesis, the Old Testament prophets, and the writings of the Apostles; without a suspicion of the irreverence of the practice, he will expand an utterance of Christ into long paragraphs of controversial matter, contained within inverted commas, as if Jesus had dictated all that Maurice is saying. He did not know that many young Congregationalists were passing through a stage of sentiment like that he had experienced in youth, were tired of solitude and sectarianism; it surprised him to learn that they read his writings for the sake of the larger reaches of social, national, and spiritual fellowship which he was opening up to them, and for the sake of these could bear patiently with his severe and uncomprehending censures of much which they held dear.

In political and social matters there were many affinities, and even some co-operation,

between him and the Dissenters.   He, like
them, was a Liberal who had passed beyond
Whig pedantry and the Revolution Settlement.
They like him advocated the extension of the
Franchise and the claims of the workman.
They were glad that, when he was put out
from his Professorship in King's College,
London, for heresy, he was free to become
Principal of a Working Men's College, and
they gave his college what little help and
large sympathy they could.   Maurice is introduced, with Thomas Carlyle, into a striking
picture called "Work," by Ford Madox Brown,
one of the pre-Raphaelite band of painters,
the two great thinkers looking sympathetically
on while a number of burly, ruddy bricklayers
are building a wall.   He worked with the Congregationalists, Edward White and Edward
Miall, to secure a conference between representative artisans and Christian ministers of
all denominations for the discussion of the
question : " Why do not working men come to
Church ? "   The occasions of our meeting with
him thus were very rare, and our intercourse
rigidly restricted, but we had him to ourselves
in the study ; and it was in his theological and

philosophical writings that his true force was found. The rigour of individualistic reasoning was loosened when he told us that personality without society was an impossibility to thought; that the obligation of social unity was not left to our choice, but was a necessity of our very being; that no man could exist, save as a member of a family, of a nation, of the race; that deep below the judgments of the individual mind there was in every one of us the common reason, the conscience of mankind, and that the training of history had been at work upon us before we began consciously to be.

N.B.
↓

To Maurice is owing the conception of Christ's Headship of the human race, which has given modern English Congregationalists a firmer grasp of the doctrine of the Atonement, and enriched their sense of Baptism and the Lord's Supper. Dr. Dale devotes the tenth chapter of his Congregational Union Lecture to this subject, and he speaks of the "great energy" with which it has been insisted on by Mr. Maurice and his disciples. Dale used to affirm that he had not learnt this from Maurice; and the two men do not hold it in exactly the

same way. Maurice speaks of Christ as the
Root and Head of humanity, the words seem-
ing to be borrowed from the passage in the
Apocalypse—"I am the root and offspring of
David;" the historical manifestation being
founded on a primal relation; and it is quite
consonant with his mystic habit that he treats
it almost as a truth of intuition. With Dale it
is—as was the doctrine of Imputed Righteousness with older theologians—a necessary factor
in the general scheme of the Atonement; and
he deduces it from the personal experience of
the Apostles. Moreover, Dale, while speaking
of Christ's Headship of the human race, does
not apply it to any fact in human history
except the redemption of the race by Christ;
he rejoices to recognise the solidarity of Christ
and His believing people, and the solidarity of
the Church; but he does not speak of the solidarity of mankind. Maurice sees solidarity everywhere: in the family, in the nation, in humanity.
And Maurice's teaching is needed to supplement
Dale's. The value of Dale's "Lectures on the
Atonement" was felt in its strenuous assertion
of the fact that the self-offering of Christ was
an objective ground of justification, not simply

the incentive and example of sanctification; and this we received all the more gladly because we had already learnt the responsibility of men as members of the race, as well as individuals, from Maurice's "Sermons on Sacrifice."

It is impossible to classify Maurice. A hater of "individualism," he never lost, nor desired to lose, the individuality of his early training. His "soul was like a star and dwelt apart." He was one with his teacher Coleridge and his disciple Kingsley in hostility to the dominant Nominalism of the time; but he was ensnared by the *idola nominum*, and often confounded his own empirical generalisations with the Divine ideas. Like Newman, he had a picturesque and apparently lucid style, but it was obscure through the affluent connotation of his words; he was not suspected, as Kingsley suspected Newman, of using language to insinuate other, and farther-reaching, conclusions than those he was professedly enforcing. His charm lay, first, in the lofty reach of his thinking; enforced as this was by his transparent purity of purpose and his deep devoutness. The delight of his guidance made you tolerate the absence of

cogency in much of his reasoning. He lived as
seeing the invisible ; when he read the Liturgy,
men prayed ; and as he preached, they listened
to one who had "heard unspeakable things,
which it is not for a man to utter." Worldly
men were impatient with him ; the drift of his
teaching was suspected by "persons of importance," and he never had church preferment.
But they who do not care supremely, either for
persons of importance or for the man in the
street, felt the power of a spiritual presence in
even his lightest speech ; Church authorities
might try to ban him, the physicians of Guy's
Hospital, the lawyers of Lincoln's Inn, and
the working men of the College in Red Lion
Square, found him neither unintelligible nor
unsafe. He forced men to reflect ; and the
truth they reflected on was precious. You
learnt from him even if you differed from
him ; when you agreed with him you felt your
position the more secure. There is nothing in
Christian biography more pathetic than the
story of how he went "sounding on his dim
and perilous way," nothing more beautiful than
the story of his death. "He began talking
very rapidly, but very indistinctly. We made

out that it was about the Communion being for all nations and peoples, for men who were working like Dr. Radcliffe. Something, too, we understood about its being *women's* work to teach men its meaning. Once Dr. Radcliffe said, 'Speak *slowly*.' He said quickly, 'You do not want me to speak.' Dr. Radcliffe said, ' O, tell us all you can ! ' He went on speaking, but more and more indistinctly, till suddenly he seemed to make a great effort to gather himself up, and after a pause he said slowly and distinctly, 'The knowledge of the love of God—the blessing of God Almighty, the Father, the Son, and the Holy Ghost, be amongst *you*, amongst *us*—and remain with us for ever.' He never spoke again. In one instant all consciousness was gone, and when I looked up and called him, he did not know me."

The time has not yet come to estimate the effect of Maurice on the religious and social thinking of the century. I often suspect that when it can be appraised, it will be seen that his abiding influence has been, not on English Churchmen, but on English Congregationalists.

VII

During the whole of the nineteenth century there have been endeavours made to bring the Congregational Churches of England together for spiritual fellowship and consultation on practical matters, for united action in national questions, and for evangelistic work at home and abroad. The Separatists and the Independents of the Commonwealth wrote in favour of Synods or Councils. These differed from the Presbyterian Synods in three particulars: they were occasional, not permanent assemblies; they did not represent all the churches of a locality, but only those taking part in them; and they assumed no authority over other churches or even over those sending delegates to them. Their sphere and function are defined in Article XXVI. of the Declaration of Order, adopted in the meeting at the Savoy, October 12, 1658: "In cases of Difficulties or Differences, either in point of Doctrine or in Administrations, wherein either the Churches in general are concerned, or any one Church in their Peace, Union, and Edification, or any Member or Members of any Church are injured in, or by any proceeding in

Censures, not agreeable to Truth and Order : it is according to the mind of Christ, that many Churches holding communion together, do by their Messengers meet in a Synod or Councel, to consider and give their advice in, or about that matter in difference, to be reported to all the Churches concerned ; Howbeit these Synods so assembled are not entrusted with any Church-Power, properly so called, or with any Jurisdiction over the Churches themselves, to exercise any Censures, either over any Churches or Persons, or to impose their determinations on the Churches or Officers."

We have not held such synods ; the absence of the Advisory Council differentiates English from American Congregationalists. The weariness of ecclesiastical debate which characterised the eighteenth century in England generally had much to do with this. There was also a fear that even the most carefully guarded councils would gradually encroach on the independency of the Churches. The religious needs of the population at large have, however, so pressed upon our consciences and our hearts that even suspicion of dangers to Congregational liberty has given way. Local meetings

of ministers led to the formation of County
Unions of Churches for the help of necessitous
congregations and for home missionary work.
Out of these grew the Congregational Union
of England and Wales, which was founded in
1831. It was at first attempted to make this
a body directly representative of the County
Unions, but the attempt broke down, so great
was the fear lest the Union should become a
court of higher jurisdiction, occupying the same
relation to County Unions and Churches as
the Presbyterian General Assembly sustains
to Synods and Presbyteries and Congregations.
It was found hurtful to the peace of the Union
to have reports of the various Congregational
Missionary Societies presented to it; our
Home Missionary Society, our Colonial Missionary Society, our Irish Evangelical Society were
severed from the Union; we would not even
have newspapers and magazines as official
organs of the Union. The Union has proved
to be a powerful Congress; its utterances on
public questions represent the mind of the
denomination, and affect public thought. Now
it is this suspicious habit, this jealousy of intrusion on the freedom of the Churches, as if

they were unable to guard it for themselves, which has broken down. The religious needs of England are calling for united action as well as spiritual communion; and it is thought a futile and inconsequent policy for the Churches to entrust to competing religious societies powers which they deny to the representatives of the Churches gathered in National Assembly. The Congregational Union has just begun to consider the question of organising the forces of the Churches. That question will bring on another—the organisation of the Churches themselves. The demand is made by some that the Churches should consolidate themselves into a great National Congregational Church. I much question the wisdom of this demand; my study of our whole history, primitive and modern, as well as the Congregational habit, makes me hold by Article VI. of the Savoy Declaration of Order: "Besides these particular Churches, there is not instituted by Christ any Church more extensive or Catholique entrusted with power for the administration of his Ordinances, or the execution of any authority in his name." But I am heartily at one with those who believe that national religious needs demand a

National Council with power to administer its own resolutions; and I think it would be quite within our wisdom to devise a scheme which, while rigidly safeguarding the autonomy of the Churches in all which concerns their congregational life, should also make the Union autonomous in all the larger matters committed to its charge.

Congregationalism has felt the influence of other considerations which have converted the nation from an exclusive individualism to the doctrine that the individual is subordinate to the society, that as he is its offspring and its beneficiary, so must he be its ministering servant, its sympathising member, suffering with it, rejoicing with it, one with it to live and die. The needs of the poor, the sorrows of the feeble, the disadvantage of the weak have made us see that competition is only one of the laws, a very rudimentary law, of life. And the doctrine of evolution, teaching us that the individual is as a wave—a living wave—rising out of the ocean—the living ocean—of organised being, sinking back into it, not, as we believe, to lose personality, rather perhaps to add to his own consciousness the consciousness of the whole, has completely changed, for every one of us, the attitude and element of thought. But my theme in these Lectures is specific—the relation of our Churches to the Church at large and to the nation ; the way in which English Congregationalists have come to apprehend the problem suggested by the words of Archbishop Sandys when he contrasts the state of a small private church and that of a great, complex, and growing nation.

LECTURE VI

SEVENTEENTH CENTURY INDEPENDENTS AND TWENTIETH CENTURY CONGREGATIONALISTS

Louis du Moulin—"Conformity of the Independents to the Primitive Christians"—Advantage of Small Congregations—Independents not "Lazy Separatists"—Orthodoxy of Independents—Catholic Temper of Independents—Freedom of Method—Preference of the Christian Commonalty for Congregationalism — Independency unfavourable to Heresy, to Spiritual Tyranny, to Faction—Du Moulin's Arguments have Ceased to be Relevant—Foresight of the Separatists—Romanism—Erastianism—Mr. Arthur Balfour—No Freedom in Church of England—Debt of Congregationalists to Established Church—"Half-Way Covenant" in America—Congregationalism an Established Church—No "Half-Way" Policy in England—Congregationalists and Baptists—Modern Conception of Catholicity—Necessity of Denominational Differences—History of the Word "Toleration" — Federation of the Evangelical Free Churches — Denominational Churches—Are they according to the Will of Christ?—Condition of the People of England—Relation of this Question to Free Church Federation—Congregationalism a Receiver as well as a Dispenser of Religious Impulse.

LECTURE VI

SEVENTEENTH CENTURY INDEPENDENTS AND TWENTIETH CENTURY CONGREGATIONALISTS

On the 4th and 5th of October 1680 Gilbert Burnet, Bishop of Salisbury, was an anxious visitor in the chamber of a dying man, in the parish of St. Paul's, Covent Garden. The dying man was Louis du Moulin, son of the renowned French Protestant, and antagonist of Bossuet, Peter du Moulin. Louis had settled in England as a physician. Being a man of some reading, he was appointed Camden Professor of History, in Oxford, in place of Robert Waring, by the Parliamentary Committee for reforming the University. He lost his Chair at the Restoration, and went to London, where he resided for the rest of his life, watching the controversies of the time with much zest, and occasionally joining in them. He was not a peaceful man; he had been brought up in an atmosphere of controversy; he knew what a clever arguer he was, and his writings are full of sharp personal invective. When he felt his end drawing near, he sent for Dr. Burnet, who reminded him of his bitterness, and urged him to make amends. Dr. Burnet himself wrote a paper expressive of regret, which Du Moulin adopted as his own. He sent conciliatory messages to the Dean of St. Paul's and the Dean of Windsor. He also asked to see the Rector of his parish, Dean Patrick. The Dean supposed he had come to listen to a retractation of opinions, and Du Moulin only withdrew the personal charges he had made. This he did frankly and fully, signing copies of confession for circulation after his death, declaring that he was ready, if need were, to write his name in his heart's blood. He died sixteen days after, and Dean Patrick committed his body to the grave.

In the early part of the same year there was published a small pamphlet by Louis du Moulin, entitled "The Conformity of the Discipline and Government of the Independents to that of the Ancient Primitive Christians." It is a clever pamphlet, without personality, and has come down to us unaffected by his dying expressions of regret. Bossuet, in a work written against the French Protestants, had made this point —the Consistorial Government of a National Church, such as the Calvinists desire, needs infallibility to be safe ; and the Consistory, so far from assuming to be infallible, rejects the idea of Church Infallibility altogether. The English Independents, Bossuet added, are more consistent than you. Louis du Moulin, who did not love the English Presbyterians, saw his opportunity, and wrote his book. He makes the renowned Bishop of Condom a defender of Independency. His argument is that the Independents, undertaking no charge more exacting than the government of a gathered Church, do not need infallibility ; their responsibility is within the compass of a small fellowship of serious Christians, under the guidance of the Holy Spirit. He further testifies that the English Independents were exemplifying their system in such a way as to be examples to other churches.

Louis was not an Independent, though Anthony Wood calls him so—" a fiery, violent and hot-headed Independent, a cross and ill-

tempered man." He himself tells us that he is
a member of the French Reformed Church, and
declares his loyalty to the communion of his
birth. But he was much interested in the
London Congregational Churches, and greatly
admired Dr. Owen, whom he knew, and whose
ministry he frequently attended. Because he is
not an Englishman, because he is not an Independent, and because he is a physician, he claims
to be a singularly unprejudiced witness. He
has somewhat overrated his impartiality ; but
his book is full of curious first-hand knowledge.
It is a contemporary record, by an outsider not
predisposed to admiration, of the life of the
Independent Churches as they were, under the
later toleration of Charles II. Those who do
not appreciate his arguments may listen to his
evidence ; especially as his narrative is vivid,
and charged with the feeling of the time and
place he is dealing with.

He shews us, for instance, the small congregations which scholarly and venerable men like
Dr. Owen found a sufficient sphere for the
exercise of their great powers. The pastors of
Independent Churches have congregations of
not, " at the most, above two hundred persons,"

and they are "eased and helped by their
coadjutors in the work of the holy ministry."
He declares small congregations to be more in
harmony with Primitive times than the large
parish assemblies in which the popular Presbyterian preachers of the Commonwealth had
delighted.   The fruit of such preaching, he says,
"was like to that of which S. Chrisostome
speaks in one of his homilies, which resembles
the water that is thrown in Buckets upon a
great number of Bottles, which have a strait
neck, and where there goes in but a few drops,
whereas the fruit of the exhortations which are
made in private to a few, is the effect of him,
who having taken the bottles, will fill them by
degrees, one after another."

He vindicates the ministers from the charge
of being "lazy Separatists," so swallowed up in
small congregational cares as to have lost the
sense of responsibility for a public ministry.
"As to the objection that is made against them,
that in case there should be no other ecclesiastical establishment in a kingdom than theirs,
the three-fourths of the Inhabitants would live
in great negligence, and in gross ignorance of
Religion.   To that they say, that their way does

not exempt Pastors from attending upon the office of their ministry, at all times and places, both within and without their particular Congregations, and to take the same pains as the Presbyterian ministers do, for what respects the preaching of the Word in the most Publick places."

He has a French Protestant's delight in Calvinistic doctrinal orthodoxy, and affirms that the Savoy Declaration of Faith is superior to the Westminster Confession, on which it is founded ; stands, indeed, at the very top of the Protestant symbols for soundness and clearness of doctrinal testimony.

He bears witness to the Catholicity of temper in the Independents. " 'Tis very rarely seen that any one of the congregation does not love all good men of what Communion soever they be, and that they do not speak of them as of the true Churches of Jesus Christ." Their separation, he says, " is not an absolute and entire abandoning of the profession of the doctrine and life of those who follow the Religion of their Country ; but of those who condemn that carriage, that doctrine and discipline, which retained the most of the Apostolical."

He affirms their indifference to uniformity of discipline in their several churches. There were persons then, as there are persons now, doubting if there can be union without rigid system, and curiously asking: "What is the Order practised among the Independents?" Du Moulin replies: "As they profess a perfect harmony among themselves; so likewise they do not believe this same absolute necessity as to that which concerns discipline. Their order is to do all things decently and in order." He refers on this point to Article VIII. of the Savoy Declaration of Order.[1]

He testifies to the decided preference of the Christian commonalty for a free Congregational method over a rigid Presbyterian government. He refers to the hostility of the people of Geneva to Calvin's rule; and says that it has been seen in England for the last forty years

---

[1] "The Members of these Churches are Saints by Calling, visibly manifesting and evidencing (in and by their profession and walking) their obedience unto that Call of Christ, who being further known to each other by their confession of the Faith wrought in them by the power of God, declared by themselves or otherwise manifested, do willingly consent to walk together according to the appointment of Christ, giving up themselves to the Lord, and to one another by the will of God in professed subjection to the Ordinances of the Gospel."

that the people have had a greater inclination to the Congregational way than the pastors. "For of more than six-score persons, who made up the Assembly of Ministers, there was above a hundred of them for the Presbyterian government, and about eight or ten for the Congregational way, and two only, Coleman and Lightfoot, for the opinion of Erastus. Yet, nevertheless, when it came to the execution and practice, there was not one of ten thousand people that would submit to the Presbyterian government. And one of them, who was the most eminent, confessed to me, that being pastor of the greatest parish in London, he was never able to establish in it a consistory, nor find any that would be of it but a pitiful Scotch Taylor. This difficulty was not seen as to the Congregational way, for whereas only the pastors were for the Presbyterian way, there were proportionably, as many people as ministers, who joined in the Assemblies of the Congregational way. Which they did with more heat and fervour than the Parliament would have had them; insomuch that they were forced to publish a Declaration, by which they exhorted the people to put off the gathering of Churches till the Parliament had made a more public regulation thereof."

He declares also the futility of the policy of conciliating the Roman Catholics of England to the Establishment by truncating the Reformation. The nearness of affinity of the two Churches "has rather sharpened and embittered the spirits and tempers of those of [the Roman] communion, to plot against the sacred person of the King, and against his government, than it has any ways sweetened them."

Dilating on his main theme—the dangers of a National Church, and consistorial government, where there is no infallibility—he points out, in three particular examples, the comparative freedom from these dangers of Independent or Congregational Churches.

There is the danger of Heresy. If a national council should err, he says, as Church councils have erred and may err, the mistake becomes as widespread and as enduring as the Church ; but it is impossible that a number of Independent Churches should all depart from the faith together, and those which remain true preserve the faith, which will spread from them as centres.

There is the danger of injustice to the individual member of the Church. Du Moulin is not favourable to Excommunication, and he regrets that the Independent Churches profess the power to excommunicate. But he points out that practically their excommunication is only the withdrawal of the Church from fellowship with a member; and that the mischief of excommunication among Independents is very small, for it is not exclusion from a large body, covering a nation; but only from a few people.

He speaks also of the danger to the State which may arise from the hostile action of a large and compact National Church within it —the danger of the *imperium in imperio*— and affirms that the nation has nothing to fear from small Independent religious societies. Their power of mischief, if they should be disposed to faction, is at most only local and temporary; whereas the authority of a great compact spiritual community may vie with that of King and Parliament.

I

I have dwelt somewhat at length on Du Moulin and his little pamphlet, because, for two hundred years, his arguments were employed by Congregationalists. He had learnt them, probably, from Dr. Owen and others; there is not one of them which I have not heard, again and again, on Independent platforms. They are arguments which have influenced the thought of the nation. Similar pleas, in favour of liberty and a free press, used to be employed by Whig politicians, and some of them appear, with a slight change of form, in John Stuart Mill's Treatise on Liberty. We do not often hear them now; their old-world flavour appears as we read the quotations. They have not lost their cogency; given circumstances like those under which they were formulated, they would awaken the old interest and achieve new victories. Their relevancy is gone because they have accomplished their work. The place once held by them as commendations of the Congregational polity is now taken by appeals to the sentiment of catholicity and zeal for the national efficiency of the Churches.

P

II

When we contemplate the whole history of the Churches in England, of which I have given you a few detached, but typical, instances, we are struck with the foresight of the Separatists. They dreaded two things: the recrudescence of Roman error, and the Erastianism of the National policy. "The little cross in the Queen's closet," which Jewel thought of ill omen, has indeed been drawn into a precedent. The crucifix is found as an object of adoration in many of the parish churches; the stations of our Lord's passion are on the pillars; the worship of the mass is restored, and prayers for the dead are invited; the practice of confession troubles many a home; the Daily Prayers and the Litany are mumbled, so that the English service is no longer rendered in a language "understanded of the people"; in many churches it would be hard for an ordinary worshipper to know if he were assisting at an Anglican or a Roman service. The very name Protestant is repudiated; as an instrument of the Reformed religion, the Established Church has conspicuously failed. "There are some persons calling themselves members of

the Church of England," Mr. Balfour said, in
September last, to a Protestant deputation,
"who seem to me to differ so little in their
doctrine from the Church of Rome that their
secession from the Church of England might
perhaps be no very serious loss to our communion."

At the same time Mr. Balfour acknowledged
that the difficulty of applying the law was such
that those persons could not be put out of the
Church of England. We may add that there is
not any compelling motive for them to secede.
The deputation Mr. Balfour was addressing had
asked for an improved method of enforcing the
law ; and he told them "there is a vast body of
opinion in the Church—a vast body of High
Church opinion—which has a perfect right to
be in the Church, and which none of you wish
to exclude from the Church, but which would
be profoundly horrified, or might be profoundly
horrified, at the general trend and tendency of
the litigation which might be set up by any
great change of the law such as you propose."
And then he makes this striking assertion :
"There is apt to be in any great accession of
strength to merely lay and legal tribunals an

appearance of Erastianism—to use the old-fashioned phrase—an appearance of making religious doctrine depend merely on lawyers, judges, and advocates, which is profoundly repellent, I think, probably to every man in this room, and is certainly profoundly repellent to the great Fathers of the Reformation. They of all men in the world would have objected to seeing the living Church subjected to anything like the dead hand of a mere technical and legal interpretation, by technical lawyers, of printed or written documents. And though the law must be there, though the law must be efficient, it would be a great disaster for the Church, a great disaster for religion, if it were brought in as the ordinary day-by-day method of preserving discipline in the Church, as the ordinary machinery of Church government." [1]

This is a frank and manly declaration of the straits in which the Protestant party in the Church of England—the overwhelming majority of the Church as well as of the nation—is involved because of the Elizabethan settlement,

---

[1] These quotations have not had Mr. Balfour's revision. They are taken from a Report in the *Manchester Guardian* of October 1st, 1900.

confirmed by the Act of Uniformity. Mr.
Balfour's declaration rules out of the number
of the "great Fathers of the Reformation"
Whitgift and Elizabeth's Bishops; it discredits
Elizabeth herself and her statesmen; for they
deliberately laid the Church of England on an
Erastian foundation. The Church, according
to Hooker, is the nation in its religious aspect.
Fellowship with the Church of England is the
legal right of every baptized English person who
has not been excommunicated. And because
excommunication is the taking away of a legal
right, and because the courts of law would be
entitled, on appeal, to review the pleadings and
decide the case, it is almost never resorted to.
Not many years ago, a man and his wife, who
had been repelled from the communion in their
parish church, on grounds of patent heresy,
appealed to a court of law, and the incumbent
was ordered to admit them. There are hundreds
of English clergymen who believe that another
marriage of a divorced person, during the lifetime of the second party, is contrary to the law
of Christ; and who publish that they will not
administer the communion to persons so married.

But they could not help themselves ; the law would compel them.

The Church of England has no right of revision of Canons, or of adapting its constitution to new conditions of the national life ; the fear of the length to which reform would go, and the direction it might take, is too great. Convocation cannot meet except when Parliament is sitting, and by summons of the Crown. Whatever the state of business, it has to rise when Parliament is prorogued. No Act of Convocation is valid until it has been laid before Parliament, and received the sanction of the Crown ; and so Convocation seldom acts at all. It confines itself to questions which do not involve much public discussion.

Of course all this is shocking to the conscience of the community ; it is so shocking that even Nonconformists refrain, in controversy, from parading the facts. The Congregational doctrine of Church membership—that it implies personal faith in the Lord Jesus Christ; purity of life ; a general harmony of religious sentiment between each member and the Church as a whole —has leavened the nation. " The appearance of Erastianism," to use Mr. Balfour's words,

" is profoundly repellent" to nearly every one ;
and the Church of England must be Erastian
so long as it is established.

III

Here is an illustration of the wise foresight
of the fathers of English Congregationalism in
the sixteenth and seventeenth centuries. But
they did not apprehend, they could not have
foreseen, how the existence of the Establishment
facilitated their working out of their own doctrines. They attributed the purity and peace of
their Churches entirely to the excellence of their
own method, without observing how the operation of this was affected by the coexistence of
other Churches with different traditions.

The most important, though not the most
conspicuous, difference between English and
American Congregationalists results from the
fact that the Congregationalism of Massa-
chusetts and Connecticut, which settled the
type of American Congregationalism, was the
public religious profession of these two states,
was, in fact, until far into the nineteenth
century, a State-established Church.

Dr. George Leon Walker has described one of the conditions under which "the Half-way Covenant" was introduced into the New England Churches, and the religious declension which was its consequence. With Thomas Hooker's principle that "Visible Saints are the matter" and "confederation the form" by which only a true church can be constituted, "was associated the additional doctrine that the children of confederated saints were themselves also church-members and saints; and of course that their children also would be so in their turn. This did well enough so long as the children of the first covenanting parents were children, and the question of their saintliness remained a hypothetical matter. But how when they grew up to manhood and womanhood, and were consciously and visibly no saints at all, in that interior and self-scrutinising sense which was generally admitted as necessary to eternal life? Where did such people stand?" [1]

This difficulty was complicated with another. The states legislated for the suppression of im-

[1] "Some Aspects of the Religious Life of New England," Carew Lecture, by George Leon Walker, D.D. Silver, Burdett & Co., New York, 1897. P. 61.

moralities, and the Congregational Churches were the teachers as to what the moral life was; the selectmen were directed to see that families were provided with Bibles, orthodox catechisms, and "other good books of practical godliness, viz., such as treat on, encourage and duly prepare for the right attendance on that great duty, the Lord's Supper."[1]

Association with a Church was a badge of respectability, even after it ceased to be essential to the exercise of the rights of citizenship; and the result was that persons whose Church-membership originally involved only a right to baptism for their children, came to be looked on as having a right to the Lord's Supper though they were "destitute of a Saving Work of God's Spirit on their Hearts." This custom proved so injurious to the Churches and to the influence of religion on the community that, as a result of "the Great Awakening," it was swept away.

If Congregationalism had been in England, as it was in America, the established, or the sole, form of Church Discipline; if to be a

[1] Dunning's "Congregationalists in America." New York: J. A. Hill & Co. P. 238.

Congregational Church member had been an essential mark of a respectable citizen, the question would have presented itself in a far larger and more complicated form. For English society was far more complex than American, having greater and more pronounced varieties of religious tradition and habit.

To borrow Dr. Leon Walker's form of question, the Independent Churches would have had to ask themselves : How about the persons who never had accepted the doctrine of purity of fellowship, to whom the process of self-scrutinising was distasteful, even impossible, and yet to whom to deny the name Christian and the Christian ordinances would have been harsh, or even impious ? How about the many whose consciousness of imperfection made the idea of a strictly personal profession painful, who nevertheless cherished the Christian hope in their hearts, and loved association with God's people ? How about the many more, to whom Christian fellowship and the communion of the Lord's Supper appeared a spiritual discipline ; a means of guidance into that full faith which the consistent Congregationalist requires as the qualification for admission to Church member-

ship? And how about the many more whom
not even the judgment of charity could call
Christian, and who yet might be irreparably
injured if they were made to live under a
constant sense of reprobation?

If God had called the Congregational Churches
of England to face these questions, in all their
complexity, as a practical problem, I believe
that in His infinite mercy He would have
directed them to an answer. But is it cowardly
in me to be glad that we have not had to
answer them? Hard, dogmatic men would
have had no hesitation in dealing with the
problem; but hard, dogmatic men might have
lost England for Christ.

We have not been rigidly uniform in our
own Congregational practice. The same Church
has been sometimes severe, sometimes gracious;
but, on the whole, and in both ways, we have
been consistent in the doctrine, and faithful in
the practice, of purity of communion. And
those who could not have joined with us have
not been unchurched.

There have been gradations among the
Churches, from Congregational strictness to
the laxity of the Establishment; the Puritans

were half-way men; the Methodists were three-quarters men, with an increasing tendency to the Congregational ideal. Different Churches have represented various types of piety, from the intense Independent to the non-defining Erastian; and they have acted and reacted on each other, in great public movements, in social intercourse, by intermarriage, and the birth of grandchildren combining the strains; by conference on great religious questions, by reading each other's books, by loving remembrance of opponents after death, and fond thoughts of fuller fellowship in "the all-reconciling world." Of each type there have been faithful pastors, gracious souls; in all the Churches children have grown up sweetly into Christian manhood and womanhood; and men of the world have felt the touch of the unseen, and repentant sinners have gazed on the cross with their closing eyes.

May I hazard a suggestion here? Is the fact that we have had no "Half-way Covenant" in English Congregationalism the reason why we have to-day so very few close communion Baptists? Those children, whose needs Dr. Leon Walker has suggested to us, loving their parents and their parents' Christianity, and yet not prepared to make their parents' confession, could find a spiritual home elsewhere. We have always regretted losing them, but we have not been obliged to alter the terms of communion to retain them. There has been very little difference between the practice of the Baptist Churches and our own in the personal requirement for church-fellowship. And therefore it has been possible for Baptist and Pædo-Baptist Congregationalists to come into very close fellowship. Not only do we receive letters of dismissal from each other; in most of our Churches of both denominations all offices in the Church are open to Baptists and Pædo-Baptists indiscriminately, save that, by our trust-deeds, the pastorate is restricted to the denomination; in some newly formed Churches even that restriction is repudiated. In the county of Bedford the absolute indifference of John Bunyan and his Church on this point has been followed, and the County Union is an association of Congregational and Baptist Churches. By the constitution of the Congregational Union of England and Wales, Churches where a difference of opinion as to the subjects and mode of baptism is no bar to membership or office may send representatives to be members of the Assembly, and this year the principal sessions of the Baptist and Congregational Unions have been united meetings, presided over by the chairman of the Congregational Union and the President of the Baptist Union alternately.

IV

The opening of the twentieth century has witnessed a new conception of catholicity, and the growth of it illustrates John Robinson's dictum that "the Lord hath yet more light to break forth out of His Holy Word." For a long time English Dissenters used to recall how much their impulse had modified other Churches, and their thought enlarged the national life. Now they love rather to record what they have learned from each other and from England. Long ago they knew uniformity in doctrine and discipline to be impossible; now they do not regard it as desirable; they recognise that the solitary prevalence of their own type of church life would be an impoverishment rather than a gain to national Christianity. The person who is always learning from his fellow-denominationalists is like one who studies humanity in his looking-glass —"He beholdeth himself, and goeth his way, and he has forgotten even what manner of man he himself is." The "perfect law of liberty" of development is the way of blessedness.

The Congregational Union has a Lecture established to enable leading ministers to give deliverances on important questions of Christian doctrine, discipline, and life. I desire that, in some memorial year, the Congregational Union Lecture shall take a broader form. I want to have the service of the different denominations to the common religion treated by representative men of the different communions, and the representative man should be one of the most pronounced denominationalists, not one of the least so. I would have Dr. Rogers, for instance, or Dr. Brown, tell us what England owes to the Congregationalists; and Dr. MacLaren or Charles Williams discourse on what it owes to the Baptists. I would have Dr. Rigg lecture on John Wesley, and Dr. Dykes on Thomas Cartwright. I regret that Archbishop Benson is no longer here to tell us what are the claims on

the national gratitude of his predecessor Laud.
I believe such a course of Lectures will one
day be delivered, and the place where it might
most fittingly be delivered is the Memorial
Hall.

V

In recalling the story of the efforts after in-
corporate union between the Congregationalists
and Presbyterians, which followed the accession
to the throne of the large - minded, sound-
hearted William the Third ; seeing how near
they again and again came to being one Church,
and how miserably their efforts were thwarted ;
it is impossible to keep down our regret.
A little more wisdom, we think, a little more
patience, an added touch of mutual consideration in their zeal, would have saved us many
a year of strife and bitterness. The regret is
natural, but perhaps it is not wise. The differences which emerged in England when the
Reformation was being worked out were not
fanciful, not the outcome of perversity ; they
were characteristic, temperamental ; each variation represented an important truth. It is
essential to such speculations on the polity of

life, if they are to render their full service to the
Church and the world, that they should have
room for practical development, should prove
their efficiency, should also reveal their insuffi-
ciency as an expression of the whole. Congregationalists required the practice of separation
to shew what Christian individualism can do for
Christendom. Presbyterians needed liberty of
combination to display the directive, efficient
power of an organised Church. The national
idea, too, required to have full expression, that
we might not lose the grace of tradition and
the feeling of history. Even the Catholic
Church, if only it could see that Catholic and
Roman are inconsistent and mutually destruc-
tive terms, would have the great claim on our
gratitude that it has kept alive the idea of the
identity of the Christian consciousness and the
continuity of the Christian Church. "No man
can be more wise than destiny;" let us catch
the tolerant spirit of history. The sixteenth
century, in English ecclesiastical matters, was
the century of Reformation, the seventeenth
the century of separation, the eighteenth the
century of toleration, the nineteenth the century of religious equality. Some of us believe

and desire that the twentieth century may
prove to be that of reunion. But we do not
quarrel with our forefathers, nor condemn the
past. Without the experience of separation,
the partial liberty of toleration, the successful
assertion of the right of all religious doctrines
to equal freedom for self-development, there
would have been no hope for us of a Reformed
Catholic Church.

VI

The word "toleration" has had an interesting history in English religious thought. The
Separatists talked of matters in doctrine and
Church practice they could not tolerate, and
we understand what they meant. Some things
are not to be suppressed by the magistrate, but
in themselves they seem to us intolerable. The
Independents of the Westminster Assembly demanded toleration—that is, liberty of preaching
and worship without the interference of the civil
law. The eighteenth century worshipped the very
word "toleration," *i.e.* what Milton claimed as
"the liberty of unlicensed printing"—the right
of men to utter all that God has allowed them
to think. In the nineteenth century there was
a double reaction against the word. Coleridge,

who for a short period was a Unitarian preacher, discovered that toleration was not a religion, was not even a force, was only a void that force might fill; and he quoted, approvingly, Jacobi's words—that the only true tolerance was the bearing of the intolerance of others. The Non-conformists, under Edward Miall, grew to resent legal toleration; it seemed to imply a right in some thinkers to extend permission of thought to others; to tolerate a man who has equal rights with yourself is to insult him. But time has brought a more equable mood. Legal toleration has begotten the tolerant habit in men; patience with those from whom we differ; the love of understanding them; the sense of appreciation; the search after truth by the co-ordination of varieties. Phillips Brooks has done good service by his little book on this subject. Tolerance, as a grace of character, will abide when toleration has become an archaism.

VII

The Catholicity of to-day recognises that " no prophecy of Scripture is of private interpretation;" but that any and every "private interpretation" contributes to full understanding. The National Council of the Evangelical Free Churches is perfectly frank in its welcome of diversities of judgment in Church polity and the government of Churches. There is no sinister afterthought among us, no complacent dream that we shall bring our brethren over to our way if only they will let us talk to them. We are like Chaucer's schoolmaster—

"Gladly would we learn, and gladly also teach"—

and we are equally at home in speaking and in listening. Our experience that it is possible and eminently edifying for men of different denominations to talk to one another with no thought of proselytising, to work together without reckoning up what Churches are most increasing their numbers by the co-operation, encourages us to believe that we have found the way to unity and Catholicity by federation. I am often asked—What of the future of your federated Churches? Will the various denominations fuse and combine their Church doctrines into a new and comprehensive polity, which shall conserve all of truth which each has to give, and shall discard everything which

is of sectional significance only? Will there
not emerge a new star, "not Jove, nor Mars,"
but "some figured flame which blends, trans-
cends them all?" Sometimes the question is
put wistfully, by men who long that such a
Church might be; sometimes a little mis-
chievously, as if the inevitable drift of things
would set the Council on constitution building,
and then disintegration, working to disruption,
would begin. Let me answer the question by
another—Will the United States ever be a
kingdom? Do the Americans want uniformity
of State government? Are they not a nation
as they are?

Let me frankly say—I do not think the
National Council will ever grow into a Church,
uniform in discipline, representative of a single
polity. Congregationalism and Presbyterianism
are not incompatible; and Episcopacy, the constitutional authority, for certain purposes, of
the specially gifted and experienced man, might
coexist with Congregational autonomy and representative government of the united Churches
for common ends. But history abides, and the
past lives in to-day. The city of God has
twelve gates, and names written thereon which

are the names of the twelve tribes of the children of Israel; and the wall of the city has twelve foundations, and on them twelve names of the twelve Apostles of the Lamb. You may call a Federation a Church, but its constituents will be Churches, and the Churches will be of various types.

When John Robinson and his contemporaries spoke in recognition of those parish assemblies, where godly life and pastoral discipline prevailed, as true Churches of God—for which graciousness they have been stigmatised as semi-Separatists — they were introducing the idea of denominational Churches. They did not use the term; indeed, it has not yet come into vogue, although that is really the Free Church conception of to-day. Probably the reason of this reserve was that there was no authority for denominational Churches in the New Testament. Constitutional Congregationalists used to affirm confidently that the word Church was used in the New Testament in only two senses—the gathered municipal Church, and the whole family in heaven and earth. We know now that the idea of a National Church was not alien to primitive Christianity.

Not only does Stephen speak of "the church in the wilderness;" the Revised Version of Acts ix. 31 reads—"So the church throughout all Judæa and Galilee and Samaria had peace, being edified; and walking in the fear of the Lord and in the comfort of the Holy Ghost, was multiplied." This is a most important reading; it undoubtedly represents a widely adopted primitive text, probably the primitive text. The Apostles did not think it necessary to remodel the constitution of the Jewish religious society, because in Asia Minor and Macedonia and Achaia the Hellenic municipal tradition had been followed. We now recognise that there were three primitive uses of the word Church—the gathered municipal Church, which was the most widely adopted form; the National Church, sanctioned by Jewish history; the Catholic, dear to every Christian heart. Is the fourth use, which persons have been driven into by the growth into freedom and fellowship of the foremost nations of Christendom, therefore excluded? First, it is to be noticed that men have been impelled to it by the spirit of loyalty to Jesus Christ, and the spirit of love to the brethren; that is to say, by the Spirit of the Lord, who has promised to be with His people to the end. And then it may be asked, reverently and confidingly—Is not such action within the scope of the promise : " Verily I say unto you, What things soever ye shall bind on earth shall be bound in heaven ; and what things soever ye shall loose on earth shall be loosed in heaven " ? Congregationalists of the last generation freed themselves from the notion, which prevailed from Cartwright and Browne down, that the method of Church government was among the things delivered by Christ to His Apostles, to be by them delivered to His people, for every nation and for every age. But they had an uneasy feeling that they were making too light of Church discipline in dismissing Church polity as of comparatively little moment. I confess to the gladness with which I shelter myself within the scope of His large words. He has not said—" I bind you ; " He has said, " Bind yourselves." And we are secure from fatal blundering by the virtue of His name. " Where two or three are gathered together in My name, there am I in the midst of them."

VIII

The condition of the people of England, about which Carlyle began to write when he ceased to be merely a literary man and became a teacher, has been an increasing burden to the heart and conscience of the Churches for more than half a century. We are as tired of unqualified competition in religion as in trade, we are sick of class Churches—Methodism for the poor, Congregationalism and Presbyterianism for the middle classes, the Church of England for the aristocracy. There is an honest desire in all the denominations to bring the reality and blessedness of Christian fellowship to the whole people; we cannot rest

> "Till we have set Jerusalem
> In England's fair and pleasant land."

This is the motive compelling Church reformers of various schools to press for freedom of action, and some measure of lay government, within the State Church. This has been the most urgent and the most sacred motive leading the Free Churches to federate. When Dr. Chalmers proclaimed, while he was a minister of the

Established Church of Scotland, that voluntaryism was insufficient to meet the spiritual needs of the nation, the Congregationalists and Baptists, with the Scottish Seceders, contradicted him. The Methodists went on their course of evangelisation without paying any attention to him. But the needs have proved too vast, the problem is too complicated for any denomination, or even for them all, working without concert and the stimulus of union. The Methodists

> " Laugh at impossibilities
> And say, it shall be done : "

but they do not laugh at this. The Independent specific for sanitation—let every Church keep its own doorstep clean, and instruct others to do the same—is not sufficient, for the very soil is polluted, and disease is in the air. The annual growth of population has been far in advance of the aggregate extension of all the Churches. Great towns have been increasing in progressive ratio, and the new neighbourhoods are not provided for. The villages and hamlets are under a wasting sickness, and the Churches have shared in the decline. The denominations have had little heart to face the problem, so great is the disproportion between the resources in men and opportunities of any one of them and the national needs. And, meanwhile, the sense of nationality — national character, national responsibility, national solidarity—has been growing in depth as well as in extent. Patriotism has been taking on a new meaning : it is not British lionism, nor spread-eagleism; the clamour of the saloon rises and falls, but ever there is an undertone, "the still, sad music of humanity," the cry of the Christian heart. We used to discuss, academically, whether there could be such a thing as a national Christianity ; we have learned too well that there is such a thing as national ungodliness. And to meet the demands of national brotherhood, we have invoked the whole fellowship of the Evangelical Free Churches ; we are organising voluntaryism, persuaded that it will be efficient when it is no longer impulsive, sporadic, sectarian, but co-operative, constant, an accepted purpose, made wise and far-reaching by common counsel. There is a deep solemnity, as of "the burden of the Lord," underlying the jubilance of the National Council of the Evangelical Free

Churches. In their forecast of the future there
may be perceived an increasing sense of responsibility, a larger patience, a firmer courage, more
self-forgetful sacrifice, and the promise of a rich
reward.

There has been a simultaneous mission for
England; the beginning, not the completion, of
combined evangelistic effort. Free Church
parishes are being organised in industrial
centres. It is being considered how the Free
Churches may unitedly sustain one, and in
thinly-populated districts only one, resident
pastor within easy reach of every hamlet in the
land. The motive is simple; these churches
have only as their aim the religious well-being
of the people. They know that hitherto Christ's
spirit has led as well as prompted them, and
they are not anxious for the morrow. They
believe the future is with them; they have the
promise of " the morning star."

In laying out my plan for these Lectures, in
preparing and delivering them, I have not tried
merely to glorify Congregationalism. I have
been quite as anxious to shew what it has
received from others as what it has given to

others; its obligation, as well as its contribution, to the national life for three centuries. It has had a history of strenuous endurance and fidelity to its own central constitutive idea, but it has also been enriched from many external sources. There has been no Church in the land from which it has not learned something, no great religious awakening which has not brought it light and impulse. The church system is to be estimated not less by its readiness to receive instruction from all quarters than by its own simple, sufficient testimony. If it began in separation, it has ended in fellowship. To borrow Tennyson's image, it has

" Stood four-square to every wind that blows,"

and the benediction of that attitude has been as marked as the courage of it. For every wind has brought some fertilising influence; and in the Christian comity it is blessed both to give and to receive.

INDEX

AGGREGATE Independency, 43

Agreement, The Happy. See *Happy Union*

Ainsworth, Henry, his Calvinism, 23

American Congregationalism, 231

Anti-State Church Association, 178

Apostolicity of Congregational Churches, 191

Arnold, Thomas, 195

Ashley, Mr., of Frankfort, 50

Associations, Voluntary *versus* Presbyteries, 94

BAILLIE, Robert, on the Scottish army, 90 ; on toleration, 103

Balfour, Mr. A. J., on Erastianism, 227

Bancroft's revolt from Erastianism, 61

Baptists and Congregationalists in England and America, 236

Barrowe, Henry, on the Church meeting, 78

Baxter, Richard, his love-story, 27 ; on the lay-eldership, 93 ; on Fundamentals, 109 ; "lazy Separatists," 144 ; on Discipline in the Independent Churches, 145 ; on the Primitive Churches, 147

Beckett, Rev. W. H., on the continuity of Lollardry, 47

Bilney's recantation, 76

Binney, Rev. T., on the State Church system, 180

Board of the Three Denominations, 114

Borgeaud, M., on Congregationalism and Democracy, 38

Bradbury, Thomas, Salters' Hall Conference, 118 ; occasional conformity, 137

Bright, Mr. John, and Individualism, 182

Broad Church, 195

Browne, Robert, 68

Brownist plea for mercy and charity, 1593, 33

CALVINISM, power of, 21 ; theological Calvinism, 22, 160 ; ecclesiastical Calvinism, 23

Cartwright, Thomas, on the ministry and Discipline, 25

Catholicity of Church, Congregational conception of, 192 ; catholicity of Independents in 17th century, 220 ; modern conception of catholicity, 238

Chapel, use of word in the 18th century, 165

255

Charles II., Declarations of Indulgence, 133

Church, Browne's definition of, 192; generous use of word in Puritan controversy, 61. See *Denominational Churches* and *New Testament*

Church of England a Presbyterian establishment, 85

Clergy, English Church, their attitude to Liberal measures, 180

Commonalty (Christian) and Congregationalism, 221

Compact. See *Mayflower* and *Borgeaud*

Conformity, occasional, 137

Congregationalism, primitive form of. Church government, 47; inchoate Congregationalism and Lollardry, 48; in Frankfort, 50; in England under Mary, 59; under Elizabeth, 64; Biblical basis of Congregationalism, 81

Congregational Independency, 43

Congregational Union, 209

Congregational Union lecture, 239

Corporation Act, 135; repeal of, 169

Council, National Free Church, 244

Councils, Congregational, 207; English municipal, 175

Covenants, Church, 79, 113

Coverdale, his use of the word "Congregation," 60; his timidity, 66

Cowper, William, on Test and Corporation Acts, 139

Crisp, Dr. Tobias, 116

Cromwell, on the Independents, 35

Dale, Dr. R. W., on Church meeting, 78; Headship of Christ, 202

Dalrymple, Sir John, on faction, 176

Defoe, Daniel, 137

Defoe Memorial Church case, 119

Democracy and Congregationalism, 37, 81

Denominational Churches, 246

Disabilities of Dissenters removed, 169

Discipline, 49, 55, 235. See also *Baxter*

Doddridge, Philip, 149; on Church establishment, 179

Donatism, Puritan dread of, 72

Dunning, Dr. A. E., on Halfway Covenant, 233

Eighteenth century, decay of religion in, 154

Erastianism of the Established Church of England, 23, 226. See *Balfour, Bancroft,* and *Lord Rosebery*

Erastians in Westminster Assembly, 222

Excommunication among the Independents, 224

Faction, Independency not favourable to, 224

Fitz's Church, 64

Fletcher, Rev. Joseph, 43

Frankfort, "Troubles in," 21, "Stir and Strife in," 50

Frankfort Church, drift to Congregationalism, 50; essential Erastianism of, 57

GRINDAL, Archbishop, 13

HALF-WAY Covenant, 232
Halley, Dr., 129
Harcourt, Sir William, 183
Heresy, freedom of Independents from, 223
Hetherington, Dr., 100
High Church Congregationalists, 190
Hunter, the Rev. J., on Archbishop Sandys, 9; on Independents and toleration, 99
Huntingdon, Countess of, 132; Countess of Huntingdon's connexion, 160
Hymn-Books, Watts's and Wesley's, 164
Hymns, Dr. Watts's, 152

INDEPENDENT congregations under Charles II. described, 218
Independents, extreme orthodoxy of, 112
Individualism, 182; Baptist and Congregational individualism, 184; individualism and theology, 186

LIBERAL party and Dissenters, 175
Liberation Society, 181
Lollardry and Congregationalism, 49
London, use of Test and Corporation Acts by Corporation of, 139

MANSFIELD, Lord, 140
Martindale, Adam, 95
Maurice, F. D., 195
Mayflower Compact, 80. See also *Borgeaud*

Methodism, 156; Methodism and Separatism, 157; Methodism and Puritanism, 158; Arminian and Calvinistic Methodism, 160; doctrine of the Church, 160
Methodist, Wesleyan, Church, 157
Miall, Edward, *Nonconformist* newspaper, 44; Liberation Society, 181
Milton, John, on toleration, 106; on liberty for thought, 128
Morley old chapel, Yorkshire, 130
Moulin, Louis du, 215

NATIONAL needs, Congregationalists and, 249
Newman, John Henry, 188
New Testament use of word "Church," 246

ONSLOW, Speaker, on Sir John Dalrymple, 176
Oriel movement and Congregationalism, 188
Owen, Dr. John, 218

PATRONAGE, Church and Nonconformity, 131
Peirce, James, of Exeter, 117
Penry, John, on the Elizabethan Church, 67; Brownist petition, 33
Persecution of Protestants under Mary, 59; persecution of Separatists under Elizabeth, 64; persecution by Independents, 46; fidelity of common people under persecution, 75
Presbyterian Church of England and English Presbyterian Church, 122

Presbyterianism in Westminster Assembly, 89, 96; Scottish Presbyterianism not acceptable to English people, 93, 222; contrast between English and Scottish Presbyterianism, 121

Presbyterians and Unitarians, 117

Priesthood of Believers, 194

Puritans, characteristics of, 26, 29; Puritans and Separatists, 71; differences between Puritans and Separatists on purity of fellowship, 72; rights of members, 74; creeds and covenants, 79

Purity of Church fellowship, not a Puritan doctrine, 73; a distinguishing Separatist doctrine, 74; maintained in Fitz's Church, 64; modern prevalence of the doctrine, 230

RECANTATIONS under persecution, 76

Reform Bill, 172

Reformed Presbyterian Church in America, 30

Registration Acts, of marriages, 169; of births and deaths, 170

Robinson, John, patriotism, 35; on Church meeting, 77; his semi-Separatism, 246

Rosebery, Lord, his Erastianism, 23

SACRAMENTS among Independents, 187

Salters' Hall Conference, 118

Sanctity of the Church, Congregational conception of, 192

Sandys, Archbishop, his reforming zeal, 4; his preferments, 6; his *Apologia*, 9

Sandys, Sir Edwin, *Europæ Speculum*, 20

Schism Bill, 137; its influence on English Church relations, 179

Separatism and Puritanism, 71; dangers of Separatism, 151; early Separatism and modern Congregationalism, 192

Separatists, 31; Separatists and Independents, 122

Shaw, Dr., on the Church of the Commonwealth, 85; on toleration in the Westminster Assembly, 99

Socialism, modern, 184

State Church Congregationalism in America, 231

Synods. See *Councils*

TEST Act, 136; repeal of, 169

Toleration, 80, 99, 104; Independents' scheme of toleration, 106; Act of Toleration, 127; toleration and tolerance, 242

Tories, attitude of, to Nonconformity, 134

Toxteth Park Chapel, Liverpool, 130

Trevelyan, Mr. G. M., 48

UNIFORMITY, Act of, 134

Union, Happy, 116

Unitarianism, 117. See *Presbyterians and Unitarians*

Unitarians in England and in America, 122

Unity of Church, Congregational conception of, 192

University of London, 171

University tests abolished, 169

VOLUNTARY Controversy in Scotland, 186

WALKER, Dr. G. Leon, Half-way Covenant, 232
Ward, W. G., "Ideal of a Christian Church," 189
Watts, Isaac, 148

Wesley, John, on Independents, 144; Puritanism of John Wesley, 159
Wesley, Samuel, 151
Westminster Assembly, 90, 97; plea for liberty of conscience, 98; dissenting brethren, 100
Wilkins, Bishop of Chester, 132
Williams, Dr. Daniel, 116

THE END

Printed by BALLANTYNE, HANSON & CO.
Edinburgh & London

SELECT LIST OF BOOKS
DEVOTIONAL AND PRACTICAL

PUBLISHED BY

JAMES NISBET & CO., LIMITED.

———

*A complete list will be forwarded, post free, on application
to the Publishers.*

========

NISBET'S CHURCH OF ENGLAND HANDBOOKS.

EDITED BY THE REV. W. H. GRIFFITH THOMAS,

And dealing briefly but effectively with the principal points of
Church doctrine and ritual now in dispute.

Small Crown 8vo.   Each 2s.

THE CONFESSIONAL IN THE CHURCH OF ENG-
LAND.   By the Rev. A. R. BUCKLAND, M.A.

THE DOCTRINE OF BAPTISM.   By the Rev. Canon
HAY M. H. AITKEN, M.A.

HOW WE GOT OUR PRAYER-BOOK.   By the Rev. T.
W. DRURY, B.D.

THE CHURCHMAN'S A. B. C.

THE EVANGELICAL SCHOOL IN THE CHURCH OF
ENGLAND.   By the Rt. Rev. the LORD BISHOP OF DURHAM.

By the Rev. Dr. MATHESON,

Author of "Voices of the Spirit," Moments on the Mount." &c.

TIMES OF RETIREMENT. A volume of Devotional Readings. Crown 8vo, 3s. 6d.

> Dr. Matheson's devotional books have long enjoyed a wide reputation. To the present volume there has been prefixed a sketch of the author's interesting career.

By the Rev. R. TUCK,

Author of "The First Three Kings of Israel," &c.

SERMON SEED. Fifty-two Sermon Studies. Crown 8vo, 6s.

> "The author is a past master in the art of homiletic suggestion and guidance. This work will prove one of his most useful helps"—*Life of Faith.*

By the Rev. T. W. DRURY.

TWO STUDIES IN THE BOOK OF COMMON PRAYER. Large crown 8vo, 3s. 6d.

By the Rev. A. R. BUCKLAND

AND THE

Rev. J. D. Mullins,

ASSISTANT SECRETARY TO THE C.M.S.

THE MISSIONARY SPEAKERS' MANUAL. A book for all Readers, Preachers, and Speakers on Missionary Subjects. Extra crown 8vo, 6s.

> A singularly full collection of points, stories, facts, and illustrations for every kind of missionary gathering, compiled by the two Churchmen perhaps best fitted for the task.

By the Rev. A. MACKENNAL, D.D.

THE EVOLUTION OF CONGREGATIONALISM. Being the Carew Lecture for 1900–1901. Extra crown 8vo, 5s.

> This book is a valuable study in the development of English Congregationalism, from the Reformation onwards, by one of the most distinguished ministers of that body.

2

By the Rev. ANDREW MURRAY.

THE KEY TO THE MISSIONARY PROBLEM. Small crown 8vo, 2s. 6d. ; in paper cover, 1s. 6d.

WORKING FOR GOD. Pott 8vo, 1s.

THY WILL BE DONE. Small crown 8vo, 2s. 6d.

THE MINISTRY OF INTERCESSION. A Plea for more Prayer. Small crown 8vo, 1s. 6d.

WORKING AND WAITING. A Combination of the Volumes "Working for God" and "Waiting on God." Pott 8vo, 1s. 6d.

By the Rev. A T. PIERSON, D.D.,

Author of "The New Acts of the Apostles," &c.

THE MODERN MISSION CENTURY. A Review of the Missions of the Nineteenth Century with Reference to the Superintending Providence of God. Demy 8vo, 10s. 6d.

THE LIFE OF GEO. MÜLLER, OF BRISTOL. Large post 8vo, 6s.

This is the only authoritative life of Mr. Müller, and has been written at the request of his family and friends.

By R. A. TORREY,

Author of "How to Bring Men to Christ," &c.

HOW TO WORK. A Compendium of Effective Methods of Work for Christ. Demy 8vo, 7s. 6d.

THE GIST OF THE LESSONS FOR 1902. Long pott 8vo, 1s. *Net.*

HOW TO PRAY. Crown 8vo, 1s. 6d.

THE DIVINE ORIGIN OF THE BIBLE. Crown 8vo, 1s. 6d.

HOW TO OBTAIN FULNESS OF POWER. Crown 8vo, 1s. 6d.

By the Rev. J. REID HOWATT.

THE CHILDREN'S PREACHER. A Year's Addresses and Parables for the Young. Crown 8vo, 2s. 6d.

A NIGHT IN BETHLEHEM FIFTY YEARS AFTER. Freely Rendered. Long fcap. 8vo, 1s. sewn ; 1s. 6d. cloth.

THE CHILDREN'S PEW. Sermons to Children. Crown 8vo, 2s. 6d.

THE CHILDREN'S PULPIT. A Year's Sermons and Parables for the Young. Crown 8vo, 2s. 6d.

THE CHILDREN'S ANGEL. Being a Volume of Sermons to Children. Crown 8vo, 2s. 6d.

FAITH'S STRONG FOUNDATIONS. Small crown 8vo, 1s.

YOUTH'S IDEALS. Small crown 8vo, 1s.

"So bright and cheerful, so clever and well written, yet so full of deep Christian earnestness, that we would like to see it circulated by tens of thousands."—*The New Age.*

AFTER HOURS ; or, The Religion of Our Leisure Time. With Appendix on How to Form a Library for Twenty Shillings. Small crown 8vo, 1s.

AGNOSTIC FALLACIES. Crown 8vo, 1s.

"Mr. Howatt has succeeded remarkably well in the five lectures before us. They are plain, straightforward, logical, and eminently to the point."—*Literary Churchman.*

THE CHILDREN'S PRAYER BOOK : Devotions for the Use of the Young for One Month. Cloth extra, pott 8vo, 1s.

LIFE WITH A PURPOSE. A Book for Girls and Young Men. Crown 8vo, 1s.

By R. A. TORREY,

SUPERINTENDENT OF MR. MOODY'S BIBLE INSTITUTE, CHICAGO.

HOW TO WORK. Demy 8vo, 7s. 6d.

THE GIST OF THE LESSONS FOR 1902. Long pott 8vo, 1s. *Net.*

HOW TO PRAY. Crown 8vo, 1s. 6d.

THE DIVINE ORIGIN OF THE BIBLE. Crown 8vo, 1s. 6d.

WHAT THE BIBLE TEACHES. Demy 8vo, 7s. 6d.

HOW TO OBTAIN FULNESS OF POWER. Crown 8vo, 1s. 6d.

HOW TO BRING MEN TO CHRIST. Crown 8vo, 1s. 6d.

HOW TO STUDY THE BIBLE FOR GREATEST PROFIT. Crown 8vo, 1s. 6d.

THE BAPTISM WITH THE HOLY SPIRIT. Crown 8vo, 1s.

THE VEST POCKET COMPANION FOR CHRISTIAN WORKERS. In Leather, 1s.

THE BIBLICAL LIBRARY.

A Series of Volumes on Biblical Subjects written by able and well-known scholars, and designed so that, whilst helpful to the student, they will be of great interest to the general reader. Full crown 8vo, 3s. 6d. each.

VOL. I.

THE HERODS. By the Very Rev. F. W. FARRAR, D.D. F.R.S., Dean of Canterbury.

VOL. II.

WOMEN OF THE OLD TESTAMENT: STUDIES IN WOMANHOOD. By the Rev. R. F. HORTON, M.A., D.D.

VOL. III.

THE HISTORY OF EARLY CHRISTIANITY. By Rev. LEIGHTON PULLAN, of Oxford University.

VOL. IV.

WOMEN OF THE NEW TESTAMENT. By Rev. Professor W. F. ADENEY.

VOL. V.

THE FAITH OF CENTURIES. By the BISHOP OF ROCHESTER, the BISHOP OF CALCUTTA, Bishop BARRY, Canon SCOTT HOLLAND, Professor RYLE, and others.

To be followed by many others.

By the Rev. GEORGE MATHESON, D.D.

TIMES OF RETIREMENT. Crown 8vo, 3s. 6d.

MOMENTS ON THE MOUNT. A Series of Devotional Meditations. Second Edition. Crown 8vo, 3s. 6d.

VOICES OF THE SPIRIT. Small crown 8vo, 3s. 6d.

By the Rev. JAMES WELLS, M.A.

BIBLE OBJECT LESSONS. Addresses to Children. With Illustrations. Crown 8vo, 2s. 6d.

BIBLE ECHOES. Addresses to the Young. Crown 8vo, 2s. 6d.

THE PARABLES OF JESUS. Crown 8vo, 2s. 6d.

By the Rev. A. T. PIERSON, D.D.

THE MODERN MISSION CENTURY. A Review of the Missions of the Nineteenth Century with Reference to the Superintending Providence of God. Demy 8vo, 10s. 6d.

GEORGE MÜLLER OF BRISTOL. With 13 full-page illustrations. Post 8vo, 6s.

THE NEW ACTS OF THE APOSTLES. Being Lectures on Foreign Missions delivered under the Duff Endowment. With Coloured Chart, showing the Religions of the World and the Progress of Evangelisation. Extra crown 8vo, 6s.

"As a repertory of missionary facts and arguments, this work is as deeply interesting as the style is truly enthusiastic, and we bespeak for it a wide circle of readers, whom it will assuredly stimulate to increased zeal in sending the Gospel throughout the world."—*Christian.*

"Such a work as this ought greatly to help in the evangelisation of the whole world."—*Sword and Trowel.*

"Emphatically the handbook of Missions."—*Presbyterian.*

THE CRISIS OF MISSIONS; OR, THE VOICE OUT OF THE CLOUD. Small crown 8vo, 3s. 6d.

"A book full of the right kind of inspiration. A book emphatically for the times."—*Christian Commonwealth.*

THE ONE GOSPEL; OR, THE COMBINATION OF THE NARRATIVES OF THE FOUR EVANGELISTS IN ONE COMPLETE RECORD. Crown 8vo, 3s. 6d.

"It is a skilful mosaic of the four Gospels in one design."—*Rock.*

By FREDERICK A. ATKINS,

Editor of "The Young Man," and Hon. Sec. of the National Anti-Gambling League.

ASPIRATION AND ACHIEVEMENT. A Young Man's Message to Young Men. Small crown 8vo, 1s.

Dr. R. F. HORTON writes: "I have rarely read a more salutary book."

MORAL MUSCLE: AND HOW TO USE IT. A Brotherly Chat with Young Men. By F. A. ATKINS, Editor of "The Young Man." With an Introduction by Rev. THAIN DAVIDSON, D.D. Small crown 8vo, 1s.

Dr. CLIFFORD writes:—"It is full of life, throbs with energy, is rich in stimulus, and bright with hope."

FIRST BATTLES, AND HOW TO FIGHT THEM. By F. A. ATKINS, Editor of "The Young Man." Small crown 8vo, 1s.

"Another of Mr. Atkins' capital little books for young men."—*British Weekly.*

6

By FRANCES A. BEVAN.

HYMNS OF TER STEEGEN, SUSO, AND OTHERS.
FIRST SERIES. Crown 8vo, 1s. 6d.
"The literary quality of many of the hymns will be welcome to many lovers of sacred poetry."—*Manchester Guardian.*
"The versification is good, and many of the hymns are worthy of a recognised place in English Hymnology."—*Aberdeen Free Press.*

HYMNS OF TER STEEGEN AND OTHERS. SECOND
SERIES. Crown 8vo, 1s. 6d.
"A volume of very choice pieces."—*The Christian.*
"Choicely printed volume, sure to be prized highly as a gift book . . remarkable for sweetness and the strength of its sober exaltation."—*York-shire Post.*

MATELDA AND THE CLOISTER OF HELLFDE.
Translations from the Book of Matilda of Magdeburg (supposed to be Dante's Matilda). Crown 8vo, 2s. 6d.

TREES PLANTED BY THE RIVER. Crown 8vo, 4s. 6d.
"This excellent book will commend itself to many a contemplative Christian during hours of quiet communion with his own soul and with God."—*Christian Commonwealth.*
"A deeply interesting book."—*Aberdeen Free Press.*

THREE FRIENDS OF GOD. Records from the Lives of
JOHN TAULER, NICHOLAS OF BASLE, HENRY SUSO. Crown
8vo, 5s.
"Fascinating glimpses of the strange religious life of mediæval Europe. No student of history and human nature can fail to be interested by this book, while to pious minds it will bring stimulus and edification."—*Scotsman.*
"The simplicity and austerity of life of these great men are depicted with graphic and sympathetic touch."—*Court Journal.*

THE DEEPER LIFE SERIES.

EDITED BY REV. E. W. MOORE, M.A.

Crown 8vo, 2s. 6d.

THE CHRIST LIFE. By the Rev. J. B. FIGGIS, M.A.,
Author of "Christ and Full Salvation," "The Anointing," &c.

CONSECRATED WORK. By the Rev. J. ELDER
CUMMING, D.D.

THE SPIRIT'S SEAL. By the Rev. E. W. MOORE, M.A.
Author of the "Christ Controlled Life."

SET TO OBEY. By the Rev. F. S. WEBSTER, M.A.

SECRETS OF SANCTITY. By the Rev. A. E. BARNES-
LAWRENCE, M.A.

PERSONAL CONSECRATION. By the Rev. HUBERT
BROOKE, M.A.

7

Works of the Rev. ANDREW MURRAY.

"All that this author writes is good."—*Christian Commonwealth.*

THE KEY TO THE MISSIONARY PROBLEM. Small crown 8vo, cloth, 2s. 6d. ; paper covers, 1s. 6d.

WORKING FOR GOD. Pott 8vo, 1s.

THY WILL BE DONE. Small crown 8vo, 2s. 6d.

DYING TO SELF. Extracts from the Writings of WILLIAM LAW. Crown 16mo, 1s. Gilt edges, 1s. 6d.

THE MYSTERY OF THE TRUE VINE. Meditations for a Month. Crown 16mo, 1s. Gilt edges, 1s. 6d.
"Earnest and pious in tone, simple in style and language, these meditations will be of help, comfort, and stimulus to many a devout reader."—*Dundee Advertiser.*

THE LORD'S TABLE. A Help to the Right Observance of the Holy Supper. Pott 8vo, 1s.

OUT OF HIS FULNESS. A Series of Addresses. Small Crown 8vo, 1s. 6d.

WAITING ON GOD. Extra pott 8vo, 1s. ; roan, gilt edges, 2s. Seventeenth thousand.
"Admirers of Mr. Murray's deeply religious and deeply thoughtful style should have this pocket volume of meditation."—*Literary World.*

THE POWER OF THE SPIRIT. With additional Extracts from the Writings of William Law. Selected, and with an Introduction. Crown 8vo, 2s. 6d.

HAVE MERCY ON ME: The Prayer of the Penitent in the 51st Psalm Explained and Applied. Small crown 8vo, 1s. 6d.; in superior binding, 2s. 6d.
"It is done so quietly, with such a mastery of all the motives which actuate men, and with such easy power, that it is only on reflection that we find out how rare is the gift of the author."—*Aberdeen Free Press.*

THE HOLIEST OF ALL: An Exposition of the Epistle to the Hebrews. Seventh Thousand, post 4to, 6s.
"A true exposition, not a piece of arbitrary moralising on a sacred text. But it is also a true book of devotion."—*British Weekly.*

HUMILITY: The Beauty of Holiness. Cloth extra, pott 8vo, 1s. ; roan, gilt edges, 2s. Fifteenth thousand.

LET US DRAW NIGH. Fifth Thousand. Cloth extra, pott 8vo, 1s. ; roan, gilt edges, 2s.
"A spiritually helpful little book."—*British Messenger.*

WHY DO YOU NOT BELIEVE? Cloth extra, pott 8vo, 1s. ; roan, gilt edges, 2s. Tenth thousand.

BE PERFECT: A Message from the Father in Heaven to His Children on Earth. Meditations for a Month. Cloth extra, pott 8vo, 1s. ; roan, gilt edges, 2s. Sixteenth thousand.

THE MINISTRY OF INTERCESSION. A Plea for more Prayer. Small crown 8vo, 2s. 6d. Cheap Edition, 1s. 6d.

ABIDE IN CHRIST : Thoughts on the Blessed Life of Fellowship with the Son of God. Eighty-eighth Thousand, small crown 8vo, new and cheaper edition, 1s. net; also in superior binding, 2s. 6d.

"The varied aspects of this practical truth are treated with much freshness, power and unction. It cannot fail to stimulate, to cheer, and qualify for higher service."—Mr. SPURGEON in the *Sword and Trowel.*

LIKE CHRIST. Thoughts on the Blessed Life of Conformity to the Son of God. A Sequel to "Abide in Christ." Thirty-sixth Thousand, small crown 8vo, 2s. 6d.

"The author has written with such loving unction and spiritual insight, that his pages may be read with comfort and edification by all."—*Literary Churchman.*

WITH CHRIST IN THE SCHOOL OF PRAYER. Thoughts on our Training for the Ministry of Intercession. Forty-second Thousand, small crown 8vo, 2s. 6d. Cheap Edition, 1s. net.

" A volume of rare excellence, and one which is much needed."—*Christian News.*

THE SPIRIT OF CHRIST. Thoughts on the Indwelling of the Holy Spirit in the Believer and the Church. Nineteenth Thousand, small crown 8vo, 2s. 6d. Cheap Edition, 1s. net.

HOLY IN CHRIST. Thoughts on the Calling of God's Children to be Holy as He is Holy. Sixteenth Thousand, small crown 8vo, 2s. 6d.

"This is one of the best books we have seen upon a subject which is happily attracting much attention nowadays."—*Methodist N. C. Magazine.*

THE CHILDREN FOR CHRIST. Thoughts for Christian Parents on the Consecration of the Home Life. Eleventh Thousand, small crown 8vo, 2s. 6d.

" All Sunday-school teachers and parents would do well to lay its lessons to heart."—*Methodist Recorder.*

THE NEW LIFE. Words of God for Disciples of Christ. Sixteenth Thousand, small crown 8vo, 2s. 6d. Cheap Edition, small crown 8vo, 1s. net.

"This book stands out among many of its kind as distinguished by a new impulse and freshness of thought."—*Scotsman.*

WHOLLY FOR GOD : The True Christian Life. A series of Extracts from the Writings of William Law. Selected, and with an introduction by the Rev. ANDREW MURRAY. Crown 8vo, handsomely bound, gilt top, 5s.

"This volume of selections is admirable."—*Publishers' Circular.*

Series of Books for Young Men and Girls.

BY DR. MILLER, F. A. ATKINS, REV. J. REID HOWATT,
AND OTHERS.

YOUNG MEN AND GIRLS : FAULTS AND IDEALS. By
Dr. J. R. MILLER, Author of "Making the Most of Life,"
"Glimpses through Life's Window," &c. &c. Small crown 8vo, 1s.
Also sold separately, charmingly bound in leatherette, 6d. each.

ASPIRATION AND ACHIEVEMENT. A Young Man's
Message to Young Men. By F. A. ATKINS, Editor of *The Young
Man*. Small crown 8vo, 1s.
Dr. R. F. HORTON writes : " I have rarely read a more salutary book."

LIFE WITH A PURPOSE. By Rev. J. REID HOWATT.
Small crown 8vo, 1s.

MORAL MUSCLE : AND HOW TO USE IT. A Brotherly
Chat with Young Men. By F. A. ATKINS, Editor of *The Young
Man*. With an Introduction by Rev. THAIN DAVIDSON, D.D.
Small crown 8vo, 1s.

FAITH'S STRONG FOUNDATIONS. By the Rev. J.
REID HOWATT. Small crown 8vo, 1s.

YOUTH'S IDEALS. By the Rev. J. REID HOWATT.
Small crown 8vo, 1s.

FIRST BATTLES, AND HOW TO FIGHT THEM. By
F. A. ATKINS, Editor of *The Young Man*. Small crown 8vo, 1s.

**AFTER HOURS ; OR, THE RELIGION OF OUR LEISURE
TIME.** By the Rev. J. REID HOWATT. With Appendix on How
to Form a Library for Twenty Shillings. Small crown 8vo, 1s.

HOW TO STUDY THE BIBLE. By Dr. CLIFFORD, M.A.;
Professor ELMSLIE, D.D.; R. F. HORTON, M.A.; Rev. F. B.
MEYER, B.A.; Rev. C. H. WALLER, M.A.; Rev. H. C. G.
MOULE, M.A.; Rev. C. A. BERRY; Rev. J. W. DAWSON. Third
Edition. Small crown 8vo, 1s.

AGNOSTIC FALLACIES. Small crown 8vo, 1s.

By FRANCES RIDLEY HAVERGAL.

ROYAL GRACE AND LOYAL GIFTS. Being the following Seven Volumes in neat cloth case, price 10s.

MY KING.	LOYAL RESPONSES.
ROYAL COMMANDMENTS.	KEPT FOR THE MASTER'S USE.
ROYAL BOUNTY.	STARLIGHT THROUGH THE
THE ROYAL INVITATION.	SHADOWS.

The Volumes may be had separately, in limp cloth, 1s. each.

**MORNING BELLS ; or, Waking Thoughts for the Little
Ones.** 32mo, 9d. ; paper cover, 6d.

LITTLE PILLOWS. Being Good Night Thoughts for the
Little Ones. 32mo, 9d. ; paper cover, 6d.

**MORNING STARS ; or, Names of Christ for His Little
Ones.** 32mo, 9d.

Published by James Nisbet & Co., Limited.

By Mrs. PEARSALL SMITH,

Author of "The Christian's Secret of a Happy Life."

OLD TESTAMENT TYPES AND TEACHINGS. Crown 8vo, 5s.

EDUCATE OUR MOTHERS; or, Wise Motherhood. Crown 8vo, 1s.

EVERY-DAY RELIGION. The Common-Sense Teaching of the Bible. Crown 8vo, 2s. 6d.

"Passages of Scripture are brought together in a manner that marvellously illuminates the subjects discussed: and the expositions are most clear in thought and apt in illustration."—*Life of Faith.*

THE CHRISTIAN'S SECRET OF A HAPPY LIFE. By H. W. S. Revised Edition. Small crown 8vo, paper cover, 1s.; cloth limp, 1s. 6d.; cloth, 2s.; with gilt top, 2s. 6d.; cloth, gilt edges, 3s.

"Full of bright and cheering thoughts."—*Church Bells.*

"A book that is capable of doing untold good in the way of promoting a more entire surrender of the soul and consecration to the will of God."—*Rock.*

THE CHRISTIAN UNDER REVIEW.

A SERIES OF WORKS ON PRACTICAL CHRISTIAN LIFE.

Small crown 8vo.

THE CHRISTIAN'S INFLUENCE. By the Ven. WILLIAM MACDONALD SINCLAIR, D.D., Archdeacon of London. 2s.

THE CHRISTIAN'S START. By the Very Rev. the DEAN OF NORWICH. 1s.

THE MORAL CULTURE OF THE CHRISTIAN. By the Rev. JAMES McCANN, D.D. 1s.

THE PATHWAY OF VICTORY. By the Rev. ROBERT B. GIRDLESTONE, M.A., Hon. Canon of Christ Church, and late Principal of Wycliffe Hall, Oxford. 1s.

THE CHRISTIAN'S DUTIES AND RESPONSIBILITIES. By the Very Rev. the DEAN OF NORWICH. 1s.

THE CHRISTIAN'S AIMS. By the Rev. ALFRED PEARSON, M.A., Incumbent of St. Margaret's Church, Brighton. 1s.

THE INTELLECTUAL CULTURE OF THE CHRISTIAN. By the Rev. JAMES McCANN, D.D. 1s.

THE CHRISTIAN'S PRIVILEGES. By the Rev. W. J. DEANE, M.A. 1s.

THE CHRISTIAN'S INHERITANCE. By the Rev. C. A. GOODHART, M.A., Incumbent of St. Barnabas', Highfield, Sheffield. 1s.

"We dipped into these pages alike with pleasure and profit. The writers, each on his own theme, seem steadfastly to keep in view scriptural teaching, sound doctrine, and the trials and temptations which beset the daily life and walk of the believer."—*Word and Work.*

By the Rev. GEORGE EVERARD, M.A.

MERRY AND WISE. Talks with Schoolgirls. Pott 8vo, 1s.

FIGHT AND WIN. Talks with Lads about the Battle of Life. Pott 8vo, 1s.

LINED WITH LOVE. Friendly Talks with Young Girls about the Yoke of the Lord Jesus. Pott 8vo, 1s.

IN SECRET. A Manual of Private Prayer. 16mo, 1s.

ALL THROUGH THE DAY. A Precept and Meditation for Every Day in the Month. 16mo, 1s.

"IN THE MORNING." A Scripture Prayer and a Meditation for each Morning in the Month. 16mo, 1s.

'IN THE EVENING." Thirty-one Scripture Promises with a Meditation for Every Evening in the Month. 16mo, 1s.

THE SHIELD, THE SWORD, AND THE BATTLE. Crown 16mo, 1s.

YOUR SUNDAYS. Fifty-two short Readings, especially intended for Schoolboys. Crown 8vo, 2s. 6d.

THE BELLS OF ST. PETER'S, AND OTHER PAPERS ON GOSPEL TRUTH. 16mo, 1s.

YOUR INNINGS. A Book for Schoolboys. Crown 8vo, 1s. 6d.

HIS STEPS: Traced in the Great Biography. Crown 8vo, 1s. 6d.

THE RIVER OF LIFE; or, Salvation Full and Free. 16mo, 1s.

STRONG AND FREE. A Book for Young Men. 16mo, 1s.

BRIGHT AND FAIR. A Book for Young Ladies. 16mo, 1s.

FOLLOW THE LEADER. Counsels on the Christian Life. 16mo, 1s. 6d.

DAY BY DAY; or, Counsels to Christians on the Details of Every-day Life. Cheap Edition. 16mo, 1s. 6d.

NOT YOUR OWN. Counsels to Young Christians. 16mo, 1s.

LITTLE FOXES: And How to Catch Them. 16mo, 1s.

MY SPECTACLES: And What I Saw with Them. 16mo, 1s.

BENEATH THE CROSS. Counsels, Meditations, and Prayers for Communicants. 16mo, 1s.

SAFE AND HAPPY. Words of Help and Encouragement to Young Women. With Prayers for Daily Use. 16mo, 1s.

By the Very Rev. F. W. FARRAR, D.D.,

DEAN OF CANTERBURY.

TEMPERANCE REFORM. Crown 8vo, 1s. 6d.

SIN AND ITS CONQUERORS. Small crown 8vo, 1s. paper covers; 1s. 6d. cloth.

WOMAN'S WORK IN THE HOME: As Daughter, Wife, and Mother. Long fcap. 8vo, cloth, 1s. 6d.; paper cover, 1s.

"Consists of three delightful sermonettes or essays in Dr. Farrar's happiest style. They are so eloquent; the allusions are so apt and picturesque; they are so full of humanity kept in its proper place by humour which hardly shows on the surface."—*Literary World.*

"The book is an excellent one."—*Glasgow Herald.*

THE YOUNG MAN MASTER OF HIMSELF. Long fcap. 8vo, 1s. sewn; 1s. 6d. cloth.

By Mrs. A. RUSSELL SIMPSON.

FRIENDS AND FRIENDSHIP. Demy 16mo, 1s.

BUILDING FOR GOD; or, Houses not Made with Hands. With Illustrations. Square 16mo, 1s.

STEPS THROUGH THE STREAM; or, Daily Readings for a Month. Square 16mo, 1s.

BEAUTIFUL UPON THE MOUNTAINS. Square 16mo, 1s.

WELLS OF WATER. Chapters Descriptive and Practical of the Wells mentioned in Scripture. Square 16mo, 1s.

GATES AND DOORS. Square 16mo, 1s.

A PITCHER BROKEN AT THE FOUNTAIN. Royal 32mo, 3d.

NISBET'S MINIATURE CHRISTIAN CLASSICS.

Red Line Editions. Crown 16mo. Uniformly bound in cloth, 1s. each; with gilt edges, 1s. 6d.; half bound, gilt top, 1s. 6d.; paste grain, 2s. 6d. each.

1. BOGATZKY'S GOLDEN TREASURY.
2. KEBLE'S CHRISTIAN YEAR.
3. THE IMITATION OF CHRIST (THOMAS À KEMPIS).
4. THE POEMS OF GEORGE HERBERT.
5. BUNYAN'S PILGRIM'S PROGRESS.
6. THE DIVINE INDWELLING. Selections from Writings of WILLIAM LAW. With Introduction by Rev. A. MURRAY.

By the Rev. J. R. MACDUFF, D.D.

BRIGHTER THAN THE SUN ; or, Christ the Light of the World. A Life of our Lord for the Young. With twelve Full-page Illustrations. Post 8vo, 3s. 6d. Cheaper Edition, with twelve Illustrations. Paper cover, 1s. ; cloth, 2s.

THE BOW IN THE CLOUD ; or, Words of Comfort for Hours of Sorrow. Royal 32mo, 1s.

THE MORNING AND NIGHT WATCHES. In one Vol. 16mo, 1s. 6d. ; separately, 1s. each.

IN CHRISTO ; or, The Monogram of St. Paul. Crown 8vo, 5s.

CLEFTS OF THE ROCK ; or, The Believer's Grounds of Confidence in Christ. Crown 8vo, 5s.

THE GRAPES OF ESHCOL ; or, Gleanings from the Land of Promise. Crown 8vo, 3s. 6d.

SUNSETS ON THE HEBREW MOUNTAINS. With Frontispiece. Post 8vo, 3s. 6d.

THE SHEPHERD AND HIS FLOCK ; or, The Keeper of Israel and the Sheep of His Pasture. Crown 8vo, 3s. 6d.

MEMORIES OF BETHANY. With Frontispiece. Crown 8vo, 3s. 6d.

MEMORIES OF PATMOS ; or, Some of the Great Words and Visions of the Apocalypse. With Frontispiece. Crown 8vo, 3s. 6d.

STRENGTH FOR THE DAY. A Daily Book in the Words of Scripture for Morning and Evening. With an Introduction. 16mo, 1s. 6d.

THE GATES OF PRAYER. A Book of Private Devotion for Morning and Evening. 16mo, 1s. 6d.

FOOTSTEPS OF ST. PAUL. Being a Life of the Apostle. Designed for Youth. With Illustrations. Crown 8vo, 5s.